PIONEER
Last of the Skillingers

The Bishop of Colchester blessing the waters, Brightlingsea 1924

ISBN 0 9539472 7 0
Revised and enlarged second edition
© Jardine Press 2004
Edited by James Dodds
Linocuts © James Dodds
Contemporary photographs © Mervyn Maggs
Text © John Leather, Brian Kennell, Charles Harker
Design by Catherine Clark
www.jardinepress.co.uk
www.pioneersailingtrust.org.uk

PIONEER

Last of the Skillingers

Jardine Press
2004

Thanks

The trustees of The Pioneer Sailing Trust would like to thank everyone who has contributed towards the project so far in so many ways, especially:-

CONTENTS

page

7: Foreword . . . . *by Rupert Marks*

11: The Pioneer Sailing Trust . . . . *by Rupert Marks*

12: The Brightlingsea Dredgermen . . . . *by Hazell White*

22: Maps showing Brightlingsea, Essex coast and Terschelling

24: The Pioneer and the Essex First Class Smacks . . . *by John Leather*

48: Owners and skippers of *Pioneer*

54: *Pioneer*, The Story So Far . . . . *by Brian Kennell*

98: The Launch . . . . *by Charles Harker*

108: The Ballad Of The *Pioneer* . . . . *by Martin Newell*

112: Skillinging . . . . *by James Dodds*

114: List of Deep Sea Smacks . . . . *by David Patient*

118: List of Illustrations

FOREWORD
by Rupert Marks

Head east to the shores of the Colne and Blackwater and there, among the creeks, you may well see one of the few remaining inshore Essex smacks. It's a glorious sight. But sadly there is one sight that no-one living today has ever seen – a first class deep sea Essex smack under sail.

Once there were scores of these deep sea smacks to be seen. Known as "skillingers" for their work dredging off Terschelling; a sandbank over 100 miles north-east of Orford Ness, they plied what was described as "the hardest and cruellest trade that Essex man ever worked". Registered at Colchester, they were the largest dredging fleet around the shores of Britain.

But for all the scores of deep sea smacks built along the banks of Colneside and the River Blackwater, only one remains. And until just five years ago, this remnant lay broken and abandoned in the mud at West Mersea. Her name was *Pioneer*. When built in 1864, she represented the pinnacle of Essex working sail.

This book tells the history of the deep sea Essex smacks, also the story of how *Pioneer* was salvaged from the Mersea mud and then rebuilt through a remarkable restoration programme and relaunched at Brightlingsea, and an account of a voyage aboard *Pioneer* in 1923. You will also read of the Pioneer Sailing Trust, whose role is to see through the restoration, get *Pioneer* sailing and then create ways by which future generations can experience this fascinating piece of maritime heritage.

The book also includes some fine prints from the linocuts of artist James Dodds, who has very kindly put this book together.

I'm glad that this story can be told. And I'm delighted that it is told here by three men whose experience include "dredging aboard *Pioneer*", Hazell White, "writing more about the subject of smacks than any other", John Leather and "having restored a great many Essex smacks" Brian Kennell.

The profits from you buying this book will go directly to the Pioneer Sailing Trust. So may I thank you for helping to ensure that a deep sea smack can once again be seen proudly patrolling the shores of Essex.

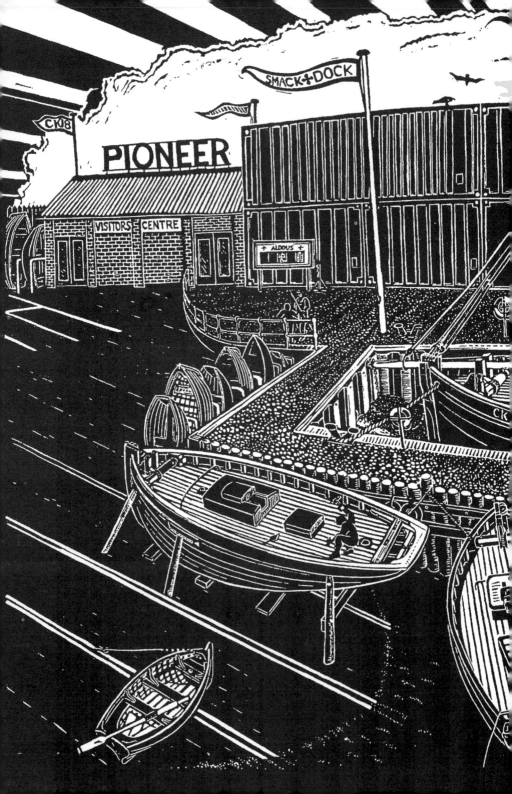

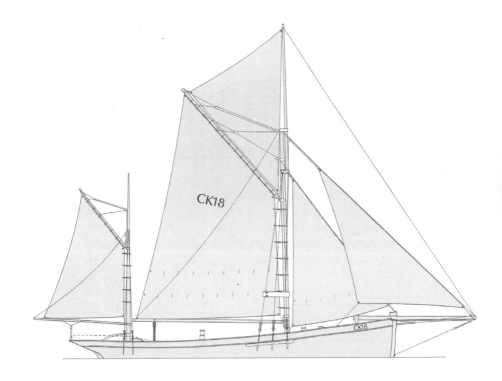

PIONEER DATES

1864	Built by Peter Harris of East Donyland for Charles Bishop
1865	First boat to be registered on the Mercantile Navy List
1888	Marked in register as broken up
1889	Lengthened by Robert Aldous to 64ft from stem to sternpost, wet well fitted and altered to ketch rig
1923/5	Steam boiler and two capstans fitted
1929	Atlantic Engine Co 35hp motor installed
1929	Fire in owner Tom Poole's shed, burning sails and rigging
1930s	Marked in "Annual Fishing Boat Returns" as unemployed
1930s	George Drewell, steward of East Mersea Golf Club cuts out most of deck in order to build a shed on top
1942	Towed from East Mersea to West Mersea. Sinks soon after
1953	Storm floods wash shed off deck
1998	Salvaged from mud
2003	Re-launched in Brightlingsea

THE PIONEER SAILING TRUST
by Rupert Marks

When we first started pulling *Pioneer* from the mud, we were by no means sure the salvage would be successful. Thankfully it soon became clear that restoration was possible, but it would undoubtedly be a long and complex project. Hence we decided to to set up the Pioneer Sailing Trust.

The Trust is a registered charity, operating strictly under a group of trustees who include Mary Falk, Charles Harker and Rupert Marks. The Trust's first objective is to restore *Pioneer* back to sailing condition following her launch on May 17th 2003.

In getting this far, the Trust has benefited from the terrific support of a number of people. Without their money, time, experience, materials, tools and equipment, *Pioneer* would remain a wreck. We are very grateful for their help.

Pioneer will return to Brightlingsea to be relaunched. The Trust has been offered the use of a dock for fitting out and rigging. This was once part of the Aldous slipways and may well be the same site where *Pioneer* was lengthened in 1889. Once sailing again, she will operate from the dock and from a mooring out in the Colne kindly donated by Colchester Borough Council. James Dodds' print (pages eight and nine) shows how the Trust would like the dock to end up – it also demonstrates *Pioneer*'s vast size.

Looking ahead, the Trust wants *Pioneer* to be very much a working boat. But rather than dredging oysters, her job now will be to train people – in sailing skills and, through these, in life skills such as teamwork and leadership. With accommodation for three crew and 12 trainees, she will be able to put to sea for up to a month.

The Trust is very keen that *Pioneer* should be available to those people who might best benefit, yet who are most likely to be excluded from such opportunities. We intend to work with life development trusts, training agencies, councils, social services, schools and other organisations committed to social welfare.

If you feel you could help the Trust in any way, or that *Pioneer* could benefit you or your organisation, please get in contact with us through www.pioneersailingtrust.org.uk. We would love to hear from you.

11

THE BRIGHTLINGSEA DREDGERMEN
by Hazell White

It was September 1923 when I shipped aboard the sailing smack *Pioneer* as a three-quarter sharesman. I was then sixteen and had been at sea for two years. As the youngest member of the crew I automatically qualified for the job of cook, as well as taking my place in the working of the ship and gear.

The *Pioneer* was on Brightlingsea Hard, fitting-out for the scallop season, which lasted from the autumn until the following May. She was a powerful old smack, ketch rigged, with a very long topmast, and measuring about 60ft x 14ft, drawing over 11ft of water when ready for sea. She had been built by Aldous in the 1860s for oyster dredging on the Terschelling Bank off the Dutch Friesian Islands, with my grandfather George White as one of her first skippers. Nobody had worked Terschelling for the past thirty years; in my time, the few big smacks that were left went dredging for scallops in the English Channel, or went stowboating for sprats until Christmas and then switched to scallop dredging.

Our skipper was Charlie Munson, and we were six hands all-told. Charlie had had his own ship the *Norman* for many years, working her in the North Sea and down the Channel. Fitting out with us was the *Hilda*. Her skipper was Jack Handley, another of the old school who had, like most seamen of his generation, been apprenticed to oyster dredging in the North Sea from the age of twelve.

Heiress CK29 on Brightlingsea Hard

While we were getting the *Pioneer* ready for sea the engineers on the yard had been installing a steam boiler and two capstans on deck for heaving up the dredges. Previously the dredges had been hove-up by hand, using a single-barrelled winch on a post with a handle either side – one man on each and a third holding-back on the warp to prevent it from slipping. This was very hard work and the steam capstan represented a tremendous improvement, but Brightlingsea boats were late in adopting it because most of them were laid-up in the summer months, with the crews away yachting. Boats working from places like Grimsby and Lowestoft did not lay up for the summer, so a steam-capstan was a better investment for them.

In the hold we had a special freshwater tank installed for the boiler and two tons of coal for this and for the cabin stove. Also down there were spare dredges and warps, huge bundles of sacks for bagging up the scallops, drums of paraffin – for all our lights were still oil – and food for six weeks.

There would be salt beef, with fresh meat for the first few days, vegetables in plenty, tins of condensed milk, other groceries and the bread. This was specially baked for us and was in big 4lb loaves, twice the size of today's large loaf. These were stored in nets hung up in the hold and if they got a bit green, as they did towards the end, you would cut the mould off, douse the loaf in water, put it in the oven for a bit and it would come up like new bread again.

By now it was the middle of October and we were ready for sea. The *Pioneer* was what is known as a well-smack, so that we could keep the catch alive for as long as we wished. To make the well there were two watertight bulkheads at the after end of the hold and one-inch holes bored in the bottom of the ship. Within the area of the bulkheads a watertight deck was laid, and from a hatchway on deck a wooden funnel led into this well so that the scallops could be put into nets and thrown down there to be kept alive by the constantly circulating water. This method was widely used in the last century when prime fish were brought to market alive. When the first net of scallops was thrown down the well, all hands would stand around the hatch and yell like mad – to frighten the Devil out.

All the deep-sea dredges had been rigged ready for work and in this state they were as much as two men could lift. Such a dredge would be six feet across the blade and seven feet to the shackling-on ring at the heel. The belly was made up of two-inch iron rings, coupled together with much smaller iron rings and laced to the netting, which formed the upper part, with leather thongs. To the foot of the netting was stapled a two and a half-inch square wooden chapstick, seven feet in length, the projecting

13

ends being used to lift up the net when the dredge was boarded, so that the contents could be emptied.

The most dredges we could work were eight, but the number that we actually towed was determined by wind and tide. Four dredges would be laid the fore side of the mainmast and four about amidships and the crew worked in two gangs, each with three men in it. Two men lifted the shoulders of the dredge over the rail, while the third man bore down on the heel, otherwise one could never have managed them. An attempt was made to run a boat five-handed, but it was not successful: the fifth man would have to run from one gang to the other to reinforce them when boarding the dredges, so there had to be six in a crew.

By the time we were ready for sea I had been appointed engineer as well – another unpaid position. All I had to do was to light the boiler and pump water up from the tanks in the hold after every haul. I often got her blowing-off at the safety valve, which used to put the wind up our skipper more than anything else.

There were two places in the English Channel where we dredged for scallops, the most popular one being just below the Vergoyer Bank, which lay 17 miles SW of Boulogne Breakwater. But before Christmas it was nearly impossible to work there as the whole of that area was full up with French and Dutch herring drifters, each with their mile extent of nets. The skipper of the *Hilda* decided to go there and chance it, but our Old Man chose the alternative, which was 26 miles SSW of Newhaven Breakwater, which brought us nearly into the middle of the English Channel.

This was a rough and lonely place to work in the autumn. We were miles outside the coastal traffic and the only ships we saw were an occasional liner bound for faraway places and the Newhaven-Le Havre ferry (which would give a toot on her whistle, whereas the liner would not condescend to notice us).

One Monday about the middle of October we left Brightlingsea a little after high water. As we drew over 11ft it was useless to attempt the Spitway, so we went the long way round, out to the NE Gunfleet, up the East Swin and around the Mouse lightship, to take the Princes Channel down to the North Foreland. The following afternoon we were off the foreland, with a nice little NW breeze, so we got all of our eight new warps on deck and, one at a time, ran them out over the side to take the turns out so that they were ready for use, hauling them with the steam capstan and thinking what a wonderful labour-saving device it was.

In the early hours of the morning, when we were abreast of the Varne lightship, the wind had backed SW and was quite strong and we really should have taken in a reef. All of a sudden there was a loud bang, and she

14

gave a bit of a shudder, so we investigated by the light of a hurricane lamp and found that the bobstay had carried away.

We hove-to and got a reef down in the main and mizzen and shifted to a smaller jib. We had already dropped the tops'l down, so we jogged her down into Newhaven and set up a new bobstay.

When the weather improved the wind was far enough around to the west'ard for us to lay our course, so when we got out to the breakwater we streamed the log, a harpoon-type instrument that had to be hauled in before it could be read. On the way off to the grounds we got a Dan buoy ready and, when we had run our distance by the log, we got the Dan over, followed by six dredges, and towed for about an hour. When we hove up we had twenty dozen scallops, which was considered quite satisfactory.

We worked here for three days, not leaving the deck except to go below for food.

If you towed longer than an hour the dredges would be full of stones, some so big that you had to break them up with a maul to get them out again. The nights seemed very long. Working there you had to put your lights up about 3.30pm and not take them down until nine the following morning, by which time there was little or no oil left in them. Our only compulsory working light was an all-round white lamp at the masthead (often obscured by the topsail). This was sometimes a job to get up into the "fork" which held it steady. Two further oil lamps, secured in the main and mizzen rigging, supplied all the light that we had on deck at night.

If the wind increased so that we could not work the dredges – before we had caught enough scallops to justify running for harbour – we would heave-to and turn-in, leaving one man to watch. Otherwise we had no sleep at all on a trip. During the daylight hours, in between hauls, we mended gear, trimmed lights, cooked and ate.

On the way back to port the scallops, which we had put down the well in nets holding five dozen, were brought up on deck Three such bags made a sack-full when we came to market the catch. On our first trip we landed about 30 sacks, which made about £50, and as we were making 12 shares of it, this meant that the boat's shares took half of this sum. So, averaging one trip a week, we were not exactly making our fortunes yet, and for this sum we had each worked one hundred hours.

We had been keeping tabs on the *Hilda*, although we were miles away from her and she was doing about the same as we were. Every time we were in harbour we 'phoned up Brightlingsea, the local telephone exchange being in the front-room of our skipper's cottage. His daughter was the operator, so between that and our owner, Tom Poole, we knew all that was going on. About the middle of December it was decided to make

our last trip before Christmas from the Vergoyer, so we sailed across from Newhaven and worked there with the *Hilda* for three days, then both left together for home, landing the catch at Brightlingsea so that local people could have a taste of scallops just before Christmas.

We had a grand clean-up before we went ashore because, since the steam capstan was installed, the smoke from the fire used to draw aft and the after gang specially used to get so black after a couple of days that they were hardly recognizable. The gang handling the four dredges forrard of the mast were marginally lighter in colour, but there wasn't a lot to choose between us because we did not wash when working. Hauling the dredges so frequently, there wasn't a lot of time – neither was there a lot of water to spare – because apart from the water supply to the boiler, there was only a 100-gallon tank on the deck, abaft the mast, which wasn't a very generous allowance for six men.

Doing such hard work, we had to live well, although cooking (and eating) had to be fitted in as best we could. Often we would bring soles or a turbot up in the dredges and keep the fish alive in the well, until we made a harbour and had time to cook and enjoy them. We'd often cook a dozen scallops per man in a saucepan or if we got big oysters, as we often did, we'd open them, put half-a-dozen in the bottom shell of a scallop, dot with butter, season and bake in the oven.

Well, Christmas soon went, and so did our money, so 1 January 1924 found us bound away on the High Water. There was thick fog and it took us three days to reach the North Foreland, letting go the anchor every time the tide came against us and rowing with long sweeps when it was in our favour. By the time we reached the South Foreland there came a nice little breeze from the NW clearing the fog, and we romped away across to the Vergoyer, falling-in with the *Hilda* about the following dinner-time (she had left Brightlingsea several days before we had). They were in the process of picking up their Dan buoy, and Skipper Jack Handley was waving his arms and shouting like a madman, so we sailed up close to his quarter so that we could speak to him. He said they'd been working for three days, and they were full-up with scallops, well, hold and all, and he was away to Boulogne.

We hardly believed him, but dumped our dan over and shot all eight dredges, since there was a nice breeze. Three-quarters of an hour later we hauled the first two dredges, and as they broke surface it was a sight to behold – no stones, no rubbish, just scallops. The remaining six dredges were also full, and by the time they were empty the lee deck was full up to the top of the rail. The old hands had not seen anything like it for years. Three days of this and we were full up, so we bore away for Boulogne with a nice SW breeze so that we could sail right up the harbour, landing our catch on the cross Channel ferry so that they were taken to Folkestone and put on the train for Billingsgate. It was seven days since we had left home and we had caught 135 bags, making £150 on the market. We were in the money.

Word soon got around and on our next trip we had plenty of company, so that the bank was lit up like a fairground at night. The only other smack from home was the *Guide*, a cutter always known as the *Jersey Guide* as she had been built there. The others, like the *Echo* and the *Sylvia* came from Elmsworth, and some came from Ramsgate. Where we worked was just off the Vergoyer Bank, in 20 fathoms of water. One had to be very exact in one's navigation or one would get into sand and fill the dredges up. There was a wreck just off the bank that must have been festooned with abandoned dredges. We ran our distance by the log, 17 miles SW and then sounded with the lead-line, the 7lb lead being armed with tallow to get a sample of the bottom. If small stones and pieces of shell came up, we knew that we were on a good scallop ground.

The warps we used were 90 fathoms long, of two-and-a-half-inch rope, laid-up left-handed. When working in a depth of 35 fathoms, for instance, we would use the entire length of the warp. The inner ends of the warps were led round outside the rigging and secured to the windlass, the towing being done on a toggle. Small holes were bored on each side of a timber-head. A bight of rope put out board through these was made fast with a reef-knot on the inboard side of the bulwark with the warp attached to this by a toggle on the outboard side.

The toggle was a piece of one-inch wood cut into six-inch lengths, with the corner rounded-off and a score around the middle in which lay a short length of plaited rope. This was made fast with one hitch to the bight of rope already mentioned, leaving the toggle-end hanging. Having shot the dredge and given it the required amount of warp, one would then lean over the side and put one or two turns with the toggle rope around it and slack the warp up so that the strain came on to the plaited rope, leaving about a fathom of slack before making the warp fast to a cleat. If one dredge came fast on an underwater obstruction the toggle would fly out, indicating which one it was. The drill then was to heave up the other dredges and if the one that was fast hadn't come free by then, one had to come head to wind with it, heave away on it, and eventually it came free – or carried away.

A dodge we used when working the Vergoyer was to make a short length of chain with a big ring on the end fast to the shoulder of the dredge, shackle the warp on to this, and then lead it along the limb to the usual shackling on ring at the heel of the dredge, and there seize it in position. If the dredge came fast it would break the seizing, transferring the pull of the warp to the shoulder of the dredge, and nearly always it would come free of whatever it had caught on, sometimes a little bent, but a few belts with a maul would soon put that right.

The steam capstans, both working from the same boiler, were sited one at the fore side of the mainmast, and the other one about amidships. The bulwarks were topped with half-round strips of iron, and at intervals along the rails were sockets into which were fitted fairlead blocks with four upright sheaves, so that the warps could pass over them easily, reducing friction and wear.

Dredges were shot in order, from aft first. The aftermost man would shoot his, and shout "gone one" as a signal for the next man to shoot, and call "gone two," and so on. There was no special working side: every change of tide we'd switch the gear over to the opposite side of the smack.

While sailing, trawlers and stowboaters normally towed their small boat. When dredging, it was kept inboard, about the middle of the deck, but right side up and ready for a quick launch if necessary – either in an emergency or if the wind was "off" when making Newhaven, for instance, when we had to launch the boat and warp the smack up the harbour. At Boulogne you'd shoot up inside the breakwater if the wind was "off" and touch the anchor down, and a tug would come to you, charging £1 to tow you in. However if there were two craft he'd charge £1 for the pair, and you'd only have 10 bob each to pay.

Life was very pleasant ashore in Boulogne, where we lay in between trips and caught up on sleep. We never minded lying there a few days weatherbound. There was a sizeable English community and the two cafes that we mainly used were the Cafe George and the Cafe Galete, kept by former English soldiers who had married French girls and settled there after the First World War. Coffee and Cognac

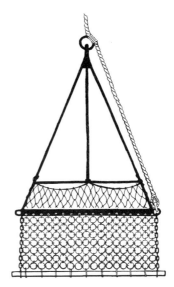

Scolloping dredge.

was 3d (old money) and French francs were 180 to the pound. Working foreign, we were entitled to bonded stores and "Old Nick" rum was three shillings a bottle and other spirits pro rata. We always had a drop of rum in our tea. Then we'd go up to the butcher's and get a joint of horse meat and roast it in the oven. It was just like beef, only a bit coarser-grained. There were entertainments and whist drives and we were earning good money, so we were able to have a good time. The only drawback at Boulogne were the rats, which would get aboard and get into the grub cupboards. Sometimes you'd turn in, and find one in your mattress (ticking stuffed with chaff), so that you'd soon turn out again and get rid of it.

A smack's cabin would be aft, with three built-in bunks each side (the two quarter bunks being exceedingly narrow and not very high). Then there would be seat-lockers and grub cupboards and a kitchen range but (surprisingly) no table. Meals were dished up on the floor and eaten with the plate balanced on one's knees. I don't know why nobody fitted a table in a smack's cabin. It wasn't as if there was no room for one. What daylight there was came from the companionway, as there were neither prism decklights nor skylight. A double-burner lamp would be fixed to the bulkhead. The scuttle-hood faced aft and inside was a ledge where the compass was kept in its box so that the skipper could see it from the tiller, but it was protected from the weather so this area became known in fishing vessels as The Binnacle.

Vanduara CK26

About two years later our local fleet was reinforced by the Ramsgate drifter *Sunshine*, and our skipper, Charlie Munson, took her.

The *Pioneer* and *Hilda* had motors installed and after this they towed their dredges quite differently to the way they had done when under sail. Under power, the aftermost dredges had the most in them because they were the first over and the last to come in being towed behind the other. Meanwhile the herring fishing was in a bad way and a number of steam drifters were up for sale at Lowestoft and Great Yarmouth. Ready for sea, a drifter fetched only £100 so in about 1930. A number of them joined the Brightlingsea fleet, were manned by local crews and were converted for scallop dredging at Aldous' Yard. The *Reflect, Reality, Orient II* and *Silver Lining* came from Lowestoft, and the *P.A.G.* (later *Pagan*) was from Yarmouth. I sailed in the latter during 1935.

The drifters were fine vessels for the job and apart from their advantages on deck, life down-below was much pleasanter for the crew than in the old sailing smacks. More fresh water could be carried, the cabins were bigger and so were the bunks, which were fitted with sliding doors. There was even a nice big table so that you could eat like a Christian and the panelling was of varnished mahogany with the galley on deck, out of the way.

The skippers thought they were in Heaven, having a wheelhouse to stand in, instead of being at the open tiller all the time. Compared with what had gone before they were really luxurious but, as so often happens just as the job is made more bearable, it fades out. The last scalloping trip out of Brightlingsea was about 1938 and then the war was upon us. There was an MFV fitted out for scalloping after the war and she worked the Vergoyer, or tried to, but by then there were so many wrecks that they kept losing dredges and gave up.

So ended another traditional occupation, one of the many to which the fishermen of those times had to be able to turn their hands. Stowboating was another and oyster dredging and crewing big yachts in the summer – you couldn't afford to be idle.

And now, if you know where to look, you can still see the remains of some of the boats that I have mentioned. The *Orient II* lies on the port side of James and Stone's dock where she was put to form a breakwater. Up at the Pincushion, where the two St Osyth channels separate, are the remains of another steam drifter, either the *Reality* or the *Reflect*. Three of the old sailing smacks can be seen up in Pyefleet, if you go there at the right state of tide – *Heiress, Vanduara,* and the *Guide*; while *Pioneer* ended up at West Mersea, not far from the Causeway.

MAP SHOWING TERSCHELLING IN RELATION TO BRIGHTLINGSEA *(c.1951)*
Insert: detail of sandbanks off Thames Estuary   *Right:* Brightlingsea

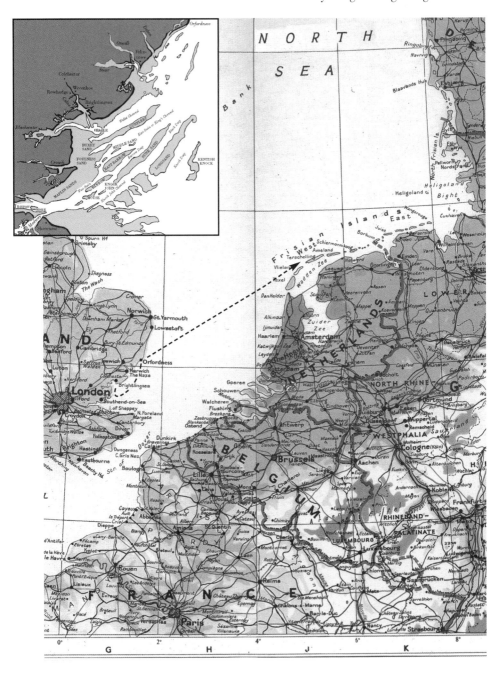

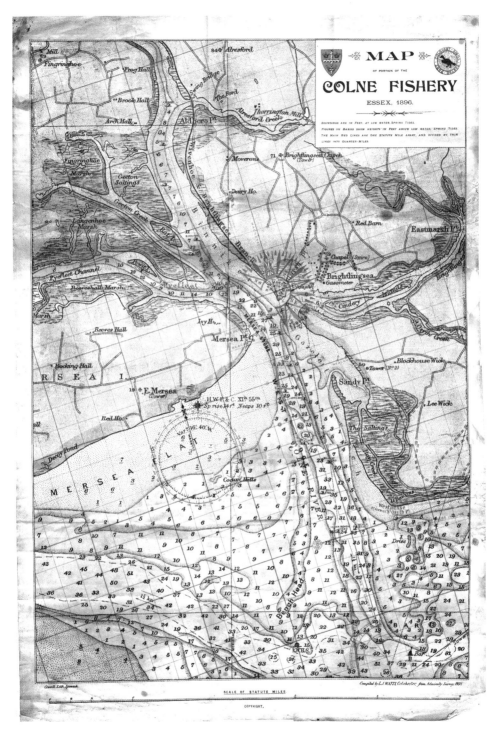

MAP

OF PORTION OF THE

COLNE FISHERY

ESSEX, 1896.

SOUNDINGS ARE IN FEET, AT LOW WATER, SPRING TIDES.
FIGURES ON BANKS SHOW HEIGHTS IN FEET ABOVE LOW WATER, SPRING TIDES.
THE MAIN RED LINES ARE ONE STATUTE MILE APART, AND DIVIDED BY THIN
LINES INTO QUARTER-MILES.

SCALE OF STATUTE MILES.

COPYRIGHT.

Cowell, Lith. Ipswich.

Compiled by L. J. WATTS, Colchester, from Admiralty Survey 1891.

THE PIONEER AND THE
ESSEX FIRST CLASS SMACKS

By *John Leather*

The story of the Essex smack *Pioneer* is a long one and she is unique in being the very last of the Essex smacks of the once numerous larger size to survive, although only her bottom and parts of her other structure were salvaged as a basis of reconstruction. To give scale to the vessel, her present dimensions are 64ft registered length (about 71ft overall length) and 15ft 2 ¹/₂in beam. Originally she was somewhat shorter, but like many contemporaries was lengthened and altered slightly in breadth to suit changing fishery conditions some years after her launch.

To understand the background to the *Pioneer* and her contemporaries we must go back to the Essex fisheries in the mid 19th century, a time of great activity and development when everyday existence at the small towns and villages on the Colne and Blackwater rivers, with their common estuary in north-east Essex, depended on fishing, professional yachting, shipbuilding and other maritime activities. There were then about 250 smacks working from the Colne alone, manned by about 1000 hands and all of course under sail

It was the building of the railway in the district which stimulated the building of many larger smacks in the 1850s and '60s. At Wivenhoe a first effect of its arrival was to encourage the landing there of sprats for distribution by rail as manure. Rumours of a branch to Brightlingsea opened up still rosier prospects – the solution of the marketing problem by rapid despatch of fish to Billingsgate without even having to work tides to Wivenhoe.

Grimsby and Lowestoft had been developed by the railway companies during the previous ten years from insignificant villages into huge fishing ports. If harbours could be made out of such unpromising sites, who knew what might develop at Brightlingsea? When the railway did reach Brightlingsea in 1866 that golden dream was never realised, but it is a curious thought that Brightlingsea might today be a miniature of the great, now decayed fishing ports had the capital been forthcoming.

In fact the capital was lacking but not the enterprise. Emboldened by the optimistic spirit of the age, many smacksmen and others who had money to venture placed orders for new craft of a size which had never before been owned locally in such numbers. No companies were created, for the thought of skippering smacks owned by these, a system common at the larger fishing ports, was horrifying to the vigorously independent

Essexmen, who especially wished to develop the long-established dredging of sea oysters and scallops which then held a high place in the diet of ordinary people, and were in great demand. This trade was well developed by them in the English Channel and many smacks from Rowhedge and Brightlingsea worked these grounds from Newhaven and Shoreham in Sussex, places partly colonised by them for some years in the 1840s into the 1860s.

The result was a fleet of powerful cutters, with glorious sheer and rakish rig. Almost all were designed and built in local yards, with the exception of a small number constructed at the Channel Island port of Gorey, Jersey, then a noted centre of the shellfish industry much frequented by Essexmen. Aldous of Brightlingsea built 36 of these large smacks between 1857 and 1867. The yards of the Harris family and that of William Cheek at Rowhedge and others of Harvey, Barr and Husk at Wivenhoe accounted for a good number, with a few also built on the Blackwater. These 20- to 40-tonners dwarfed the little 10-ton estuary oyster dredgers, and between them existed a great difference in purpose and voyagings, and most of them were cutter rigged with spars of large size.

The *Pioneer* was built by Peter Harris at the maritime village of Rowhedge, in the parish of East Donyland on the upper reaches of the river Colne. It has deep water by its quays and was the home of many mariners and shipbuilders and, after the 1780s of large numbers of professional captains and hands for yachts of all sizes and types, many of whom found something of a winter living fishing in the fifty or so smacks owned there. By the 1860s 29 of these were of the larger size, from 58 - 72ft overall length, almost all rigged as cutters. The remainder of the fleet were generally from 42 to 50ft long. Most were built in the various village shipyards, which also built many of the smaller clinker planked and cutter rigged fishing craft known as "yawls", about 30ft in length, besides brigs, schooners and barquentines on occasion. William Cheek was one early builder and Thomas Lay and Samuel Spunner others. At least one smack was built there by Robert Farrow, several by Daniel Martin and others by Joseph Cole. But the Harris family were the most prolific builders of smacks at Rowhedge, launching many throughout the 19th century. Samuel Harris seems to have been the earliest of them in business and there are detailed records of smacks and fishing "yawls" and cutters, many with the clench built hulls then common, built by him between 1808 and 1829. Some of them were notably fast, including the aptly named cutter *Dagger*, launched in 1815, which ended her days in 1835 when seized by the customs for smuggling 78 casks of spirits. She was condemned to be sawn up and sold for scrap timber and firewood. Rowhedge mariners were frequently smugglers.

PIONEER'S WET WELL

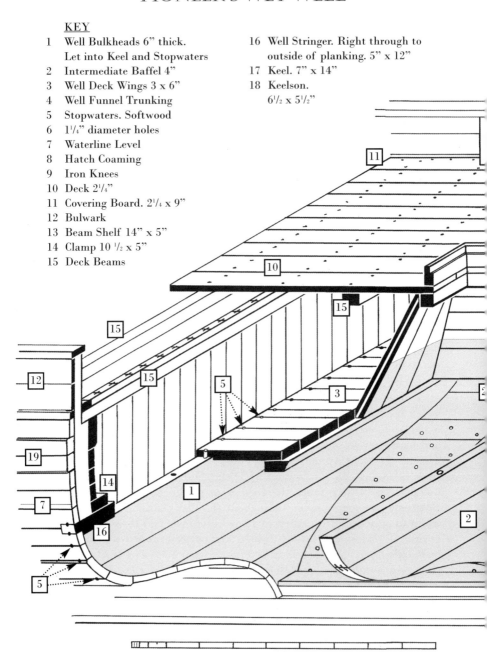

KEY

1 Well Bulkheads 6" thick.
  Let into Keel and Stopwaters
2 Intermediate Baffel 4"
3 Well Deck Wings 3 x 6"
4 Well Funnel Trunking
5 Stopwaters. Softwood
6 1¹/₄" diameter holes
7 Waterline Level
8 Hatch Coaming
9 Iron Knees
10 Deck 2¹/₄"
11 Covering Board. 2¹/₄ x 9"
12 Bulwark
13 Beam Shelf 14" x 5"
14 Clamp 10 ¹/₂ x 5"
15 Deck Beams

16 Well Stringer. Right through to
  outside of planking. 5" x 12"
17 Keel. 7" x 14"
18 Keelson.
  6¹/₂ x 5¹/₂"

19 Planking 2" and 3" 21 Futtock Frames 8¾ x 5"
20 Single Frame scarphed over Keel. 4" x 5" 22 Softwood Reads or tongues
Shaded area indicates water level within the well

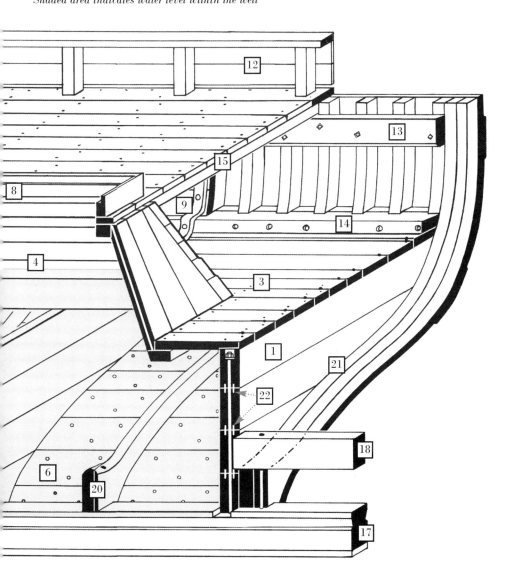

James Harris also built at Rowhedge during the same period and his first recorded vessel was the smack *Sarah*, built in 1821. She too was fast and in 1830 was also seized by the customs and condemned. James sometimes built a smack for his own account, later to be sold, and also at least two cargo schooners, one for widow Harriet Harris of Rowhedge. One of the smacks built by James Harris is particularly interesting to me as she was owned by my great-grandfather, Thomas Barnard of Rowhedge. One of a succession of smacks owned by this redoubtable Essex mariner renowned for his exploits in fishing many waters, in salvaging, lifesaving, piloting and at times in smuggling. The *New Unity* had relevance to the *Pioneer* as she was built at the same yard and with similar dimensions only five years before and was originally rigged as a cutter, with registered dimensions of 56ft 1in in length. 15ft 1in beam and 7ft 4in depth. Her draught was 8ft 6in. To give an impression of her cutter rig, the boom was about 52ft long and the bowsprit 30ft outboard; the sail area about 2000 square feet. She too was later lengthened in 1872 to 68ft 1in in registered length, about 76ft overall, and was also re-rigged as a ketch. The *New Unity* was lost in a winter gale, with heavy snow, in 1881. Great-grandfather and all his crew got safely ashore.

In 1864 the yard was taken over by Peter T. Harris who, with Enos Harris, was to build more than 60 smacks and many yachts, and to repair many more until the premises were leased to the Rowhedge Ironworks Co. shipyard in 1915, eventually becoming their property in 1943. It was later the yacht yard of Ian Brown Ltd and now a site of residential building.

When Peter T. Harris took over the yard in 1864 one of his first orders was for a 23-ton smack, with registered dimensions of 53ft length (measured from the forward side of stem at deck to the after side of sternpost at deck); 13ft 10½in beam and a registered depth of 6ft 10in. The registered depth could be a deceptive dimension as it was taken from the top of deck beams at side to the top of floors, amidships, or at times to the top of hold ceiling and consequently did not record the actual depth of the hull. The true depth is the "moulded depth", taken from the top of deck beams at side to the face of floor or frame where this meets the keel. Neither dimension is representative of the draught of the hull.

Like almost all the 29 or so Rowhedge built smacks of this size afloat at that time, the *Pioneer* was cutter rigged when built. The speed of these Colne smacks under sail, particularly those built at Rowhedge by the Harris's and others, was well known and study of entry and run of the *Pioneer*'s hull confirms this potential.

The Rowhedge *Aquiline*, owned by Captain Harry Mills Cook, was typical of these craft. A bold-sheered cutter of 21 registered tons, she was launched from Harris's yard in 1856, where her 65ft hull was well and truly built, and finely formed; having a beam of 15ft and drawing a typical 8ft 6in when loaded to her hold capacity of 21-tons, and a little less when light. She carried a sail area of about 2000 square feet in her working canvas. Spars were sizeable, as her main boom was 45ft long and the bowsprit was some 30ft outboard. When sea dredging the mainsail was handed and its boom stowed in a crutch, and a large trysail having its own gaff was set in its place, sheeted by tackles to the quarters.

The arrangement of these vessels differed greatly from the smaller smacks which survive today. Forward, the usual hand-spike windlass handled the anchor cable, which ran out clear of the stem on a short "davit", and, in season, the stowboat gear for spratting. A large geared hand winch having four barrels was fitted immediately forward of the mast for use in working halliards, running out the bowsprit, working fishing gear or whipping out cargo. A winch or geared hand capstan stood amidships and could be worked by two or more hands when dredging or working trawl warps, all of which were hauled by muscle power as, unlike the specialised trawling smacks from the big fishing ports which were equipped with steam capstans, the Essex boats relied solely on "Armstrong's patent" to set their gear, a feature of working which they endured until the eclipse of sail. A clinker built boat about 15ft long was carried on deck or lashed, capsized, over the main hatch in foul weather. In port on Sundays and regatta days, most of them sported a long masthead pennant emblazoned with the smack's name or initials and other fancy work. Many had signal letters allotted to them, which is proof of their varied sea work, but few had shroud channels as these interfered with the boarding of heavy stowboat gear. Sometimes local customs went into the hulls, for you could always tell a Wivenhoe-built smack from one launched across the river at Rowhedge, by the half round rubbing strake her builders fitted, the Rowhedge smacks having flat ones.

Below decks the fore peak was a cable locker. Abaft this the "mast room", as the space between peak bulkhead and mast was called, housed a large scuttle butt for drinking water and racks for bread and vegetable stores on extended voyaging. Partial bulkheads set it off from the hold, which occupied about one third of the smack's length and had a capacity of 21-tons on her ballast, which was clean beach shingle with a proportion of iron pigs covered by a wood ceiling.

All hands berthed in the cabin aft, entered by a sliding hatch in the deck. In this space of perhaps 14 x 9ft, six men lived for months on end. Locker seats ran down each side and the four bunks lining the topsides behind them each had sliding panels which could be closed by the

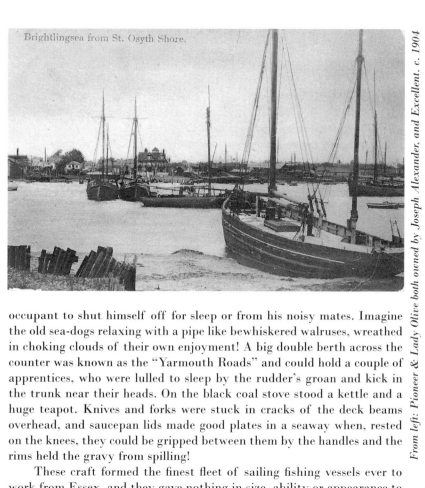

From left: Pioneer & Lady Olive both owned by Joseph Alexander, and Excellent. c. 1904

occupant to shut himself off for sleep or from his noisy mates. Imagine the old sea-dogs relaxing with a pipe like bewhiskered walruses, wreathed in choking clouds of their own enjoyment! A big double berth across the counter was known as the "Yarmouth Roads" and could hold a couple of apprentices, who were lulled to sleep by the rudder's groan and kick in the trunk near their heads. On the black coal stove stood a kettle and a huge teapot. Knives and forks were stuck in cracks of the deck beams overhead, and saucepan lids made good plates in a seaway when, rested on the knees, they could be gripped between them by the handles and the rims held the gravy from spilling!

These craft formed the finest fleet of sailing fishing vessels ever to work from Essex, and they gave nothing in size, ability or appearance to the smacks from Brixham, Ramsgate or Yarmouth, many of whom, with some Essexmen, "colonised" Grimsby and Hull. In them the great-grandfathers of many of us found their living and learned or displayed their seamanship. There is no point in attempting to glamourise the fisheries, which were always hard, often dangerous, and usually miserably rewarding financially; but that they bred men of strong and independent character there is no doubt. Theirs was none of the comparatively idyllic life of the estuary dredgers, but a thrusting existence, alive to any and every opportunity which came their way.

Most skippers began as apprentices, serving aboard their master's smack and living in his house when in port. These local boys were often sent to sea at the age of 12, being bound for five, seven or nine years to the owner, who might have two such boys serving aboard his smack. This system existed in the 17th century, but seems to have died out at the end of the 19th century. Strict rules were laid down for apprentices' behaviour when ashore. Pubs were barred, as was playing at cards or dice; and they were not allowed to marry, though this would have been pretty hopeless anyway on a yearly wage of £10 or £12. The owner found them food, but the apprentices kept themselves in their favourite rig of "cheesecutter" cap, white canvas jumper or smock over a thick guernsey, and thick duffle trousers tucked into leather sea boots with cobbled soles. It was a way of life which produced smart seamen and gave fair promise of advancement for those times. There was little of the "by guess and by God" style of navigation among these smacks' confident skippers, most of whom were progressive enough to obtain fishing master's certificates when these were introduced in the 1870s.

Their quest for oysters and scallops led the Essexmen, at various seasons, to work the Inner Dowsing and Dudgeon banks, landing at Grimsby or Blakeney; the Ness grounds, stretching from Orfordness to Cromer; the Gatloper and Kentish Knock areas of the North Sea and the Terschelling and Hinder banks off the Dutch coast, landing at Brightlingsea. In the Channel they dredged the Goodwin, Sandettie and Varne grounds, with those off the French coast at Caen Bay, Dieppe, St Valery-sur-Somme, Fecamp, Calais and Dunkirk, using Ramsgate, Dover, Newhaven or Shore-ham as ports. Down Channel, West Bay provided some work, landing at Weymouth and, in earlier times, the Cornish Fal and Helford rivers were visited – one almost writes raided – by the Essexmen, while the Channel Island of Jersey attracted large numbers of Essex smacks to its fishery for 70 years. Many sailed "round the land" to work on the south Pembrokeshire coast, based at Swansea; and Bangor, South Western Ireland, and the Solway Firth also regularly saw the rakish Colne topmasts.

Work aboard was hard when dredging. On the grounds the topmast was often struck and a reef tucked in the mainsail, or the trysail would be set to ease speed and motion in a seaway and keep the boom clear of unwary heads. After this they worked almost continuously, day and night, with only occasional spells for mugs of tea and a bite to eat. It must have been muscle-cracking toil winding up those huge sea dredges with their 6ft hoeing edges from 25 fathoms, by hand. Often six were worked at a time on 65-fathom, 3 inch bass warps leading in through multiple rollers on the rail or through a port in the bulwark. Each weary foot of it was cranked home with one man keeping tension on the slack which jerked back on every sea to etch new scars into hands already torn by the

tiny shells picked up by the warp. So it would go on hour after hour without even the respite of sorting between hauls which trawling gives. At about 3am the gear would be laid in and the crew took half-hour watches before recommencing at six, and this might go on for five or six days! They must have been heartily sick of oysters by the time the voyage ended, as, after spending all day and half the night hauling dredges from the heaving sea, they tumbled below to be confronted by dishes of steaming oyster soup!

Hard as they were the fisheries flourished. By 1874 there were 132 first-class smacks of 15 to 50 tons registered at Colchester, in addition to 250 second-class of under 15 tons and 40 third-class vessels. The largest number of these larger smacks were owned at Brightlingsea, with Rowhedge accounting for about 20 and Wivenhoe and Tollesbury for about a dozen each. Few of these large vessels were owned by West Mersea fishermen, whose interests were chiefly centred in the Blackwater oyster fisheries, and none were owned by them in the latter days of sail.

Rich oyster beds were discovered by the big smacks off Jersey in 1797, and news travelled fast even then for, within a few months, a fleet of over 300 smacks from Essex, Shoreham, Emsworth and Faversham, manned by 2000 men, was working there. In a few months the quiet port of Gorey became a boom town, with scenes ashore which must have rivalled the gold rush days that were to come. A fleet of 60 Essex smacks sailed there each spring and carried on dredging these waters despite the hazards of the Napoleonic wars, when the crew of one smack were captured in the Channel by a French warship and imprisoned for seven years. Released when the war was ended, these half starved but still tough seamen hiked to Gravelines, where they stole a boat and rowed to Portsmouth – a feat in itself, but they capped that by walking home to Brightlingsea.

Friction with the French continued long after the war as the best grounds extended into their territorial waters, and the English boats were often arrested as poachers. The limit went up to six miles in 1824 and violence flared four years later when a number of smacks, including many from Essex, were attacked while dredging off Chausey, in French waters. Men from two French warships boarded one and took her as a prize into a French port.

After this things went from bad to worse, and in 1832 the Colne boats returned home complaining of lack of naval protection when dredging. The next year the Brightlingsea *Hebe* was seized by a French gunboat and her crew set adrift in the Channel; it was alleged that the British gunboat *Seaflower* made no attempt to interfere or to assist them. By 1845 the French beds were in a depleted condition and delay by the authorities in opening the re-stocked grounds in Grouville Bay led to serious disorders at Gorey, where it took a regiment of the Island garrison to control the rioting smacksmen. Afterwards the masters of 96 smacks were fined by the Jersey government and 15 of the Essexmen turned their attentions to the grounds off Dieppe in deliberately organised sweeps around Cape D'Ailly, despite French protests. After some revival the Jersey fishery became exhausted by 1871.

Wherever there were oysters or scallops the far-ranging Essexmen would find them. By the 1830s they were participating in the flourishing fishery worked by the fishermen of Mumbles, in Swansea and Cardigan Bays, Pembrokeshire. In 1844 the heavy dredging of local grounds was arousing protests from the mayor of Swansea, who suggested the council should interfere before the beds were entirely destroyed. But, as usual, little was done, and during the following 20 years a total of 9,000,000 oysters were dredged annually by a fleet of smacks 200 strong, and many thousands of spat oysters were taken back to restock the beds in Colne and Blackwater, the Roach and Crouch and at Whitstable and Faversham.

However antagonised they felt, the Welsh fishermen were so impressed by the graceful and handy Essex cutters which were so much abler than their own lug-rigged "skiffs" that, around 1855, a delegation of them travelled to Colneside to study local smacks and methods – an early and enterprising example of work study. As a result some orders were placed with the Colne yards for small vessels of around 12 tons, which cost about £300 complete, and there was great rejoicing at Mumbles when the first of these, the *Seven Sisters*, arrived there. She was followed by many more, but later Mumbles "skiffs", as the Welshmen called them, were constructed by Bristol Channel builders who copied the lines and arrangement of the Essex-built boats; and they were in turn copied by the Brixham men for their "Mumble Bees", as they called their smaller cutters. A few years later the Welsh fishery was becoming impoverished, and declined thereafter, finally becoming extinct just after the First World War.

Another example of overfishing occurred in the oyster fishery which developed from Blakeney, Wells and Cley during the middle part of the 19th century. Numbers of small local smacks were working a profitable fishery on the Dudgeon, which flourished until 1834 when 60 or so Colne smacks suddenly arrived and began to work the grounds, to the amazed

OFFICIAL NUMBER OF SHIP _48.991_

Port Number ... _1_	Port of Registry ... _Colchester_	British or Foreign-built ... } _British_

Number of Decks	_One_	Build	_Carvel_	
Number of Masts	_One_	Gallery	_None_	
Rigging	_Smack_	Head	_None_	
Stern	_Square_	Framework	_Wood_	

Tonnage.

	No. of Tons
Tonnage under Tonnage Deck	_25.18_
Closed-in Spaces above the Tonnage Deck, if any, viz.,	
Space or Spaces between Decks	
Poop	
Roundhouse	
Other enclosed Spaces (if any), naming them . . .	
Gross Tonnage, being Register Tonnage, if a Sailing Ship . .	_23.18_
If a Steamer, deduct Allowance for propelling Power, as per other Side . .	
Register Tonnage, if a Steamer	

Names, Residence, and Description of the Owners, and Number of Sixty-fourth Shares held by each Owner · · · _Charles Ford Bishop, of Cowes in the Isle of Wight. Master Mariner_

Dated _3rd January 1865_

Col. 1.	Col. 2.	Col. 3.	Col. 4.	Col. 5.	Col. 6.	Col. 7.
Number of Transaction.	Letter denoting Mortgages, and Certificates of Mortgages.	Name of Person from whom Title is derived.	Number of Shares affected.	Date of Registry.	Nature and Date of Transaction.	Name, Residence, and Occupation of Transferee, Mortgagee, or other Person acquiring Title or Power.
1		Charles Ford Bishop	64	25th April 1868 10.30 A.M.	Bill of Sale dated 25th October 1866	Thomas Brassey of Beauport in the County of Sussex, Gentleman
2		Thomas Brassey	64	30th April 1868 11.30 A.M.	Bill of Sale dated 27th April 1868	Joseph Alexander of Brightlingsea in the County of Essex, Butcher.
3	A	Joseph Alexander	64	25 May 1868 1 P.M.	Mortgage A, dated 30 April 1868 for £110 and interest at 10%	George Cracknell of Lowestoft in the County of Suffolk, Eng.
4	A	George Cracknell	64	25 June 1871 1.30 P.M.	Discharge of Mortgage A for £110 duly receipt dated 1st June 1871	
5	B	Joseph Alexander	64	23 June 1871 1.30 P.M.	Mortgage B, dated 1st June 1871 for £150 & int. 5%	Henry Egerton Green of Colchester in the County of Essex, Banker.

51

NAME OF SHIP "Pioneer" 1888

| Whether a Sailing or Steam Ship; if Steam, how propelled | Sailing | | Where built ... at East Donyland in the County of Essex on the 22ᵈ December 1864 | When built ... 22ᵈ Decr 1864 |

Closed 6/12/88 — 150
See Reg.

		Measurements	Length from the Forepart of the Stem under the Bowsprit to the Aft Side of the Head of the Stern-post 53 Feet — Tenths.
			Main Breadth to Outside of Plank — 13 — Feet 9 — Tenths.
			Depth in Hold from Tonnage Deck to Ceiling at Midships — 6 — Feet 9 — Tenths.

Additional Particulars for Steamers.

| | | Tons. |

Deduction for Space required for propelling Power (as measured) . . . .

Length of Engine Room (if measured)   Feet   Tenths.

Number of Engines

Combined Power (estimated Horse Power) .

by four 64
Total 64

(Signed)   Rob Ragget   Registrar.

Col. 8.	Col. 9.	Col. 10.	Col. 11.	Col. 12.	Col. 13.	Col. 14.
Number and Account of subsequent Transaction, showing how Interest disposed of.	Number of Transaction under which Title acquired.	Names of Owners.	Mortgages and Certificates of Mortgages.	Names of Mortgagees or Attorneys under Certificates of Mortgage.	Number of Shares.	REMARKS.
	1	Thomas Brassey			64	
			Total 25ᵗʰ April 1868		64	Rob Ragget Regr
	2	Joseph Alexander			64	
			Total 30 April 1868		64	Rob Ragget Regr
Discharged No 4	1.243	Joseph Alexander	Mortgage (A) for £110 & interest at 5%	George Cracknell	64	
			Total 25 May 1868		64	Rob Ragget Regr
Discharged No 6	1.245	Joseph Alexander	Mortgage (B) dated for £150 & interest 6%	Henry Egerton Green	64	Joseph Alexander of Brightlingsea managing owner per letter from himself dated 15th March 1878 Entered Actg Regr 43/78
			Total 25 June 1871		64	Jos Barton Registrar
			Carried forward to Book 3. page 150			

resentment of the Norfolk men. Having almost cleared the fishery, which never really recovered, they disappeared, except for five or six who remained dredging, landing their catches at Lynn, Wells or Blakeney – where the 19-ton *Thorn*, once owned by the renowned Rowhedger Jack Spitty, was wrecked on the bar with the loss of all hands when entering that treacherous and unlit haven before a north-easterly gale.

Largo Bay on the north shore of the Firth of Forth was another area dredged by a fleet from Colne one season. Here they met spirited local opposition from the Scots fishermen who, armed with stones, attacked them in their boats. They crowded into the tiny harbour of Newhaven and slept under police protection, with axes and windlass spikes laid handy! Eventually the navy sent a gunboat to keep the peace.

Some readers will know of the dredging of sea oysters on the Terschelling bank off the Dutch coast, which led to all the big smacks being dubbed "Skillingers" in recent times. But it should be remembered that this fishery, important and arduous as it was, formed only a part of the very many grounds and trades worked by these versatile seamen and their craft, as we have seen. This fishery lies off the island of Terschelling, about 112 miles to the eastward of Orfordness, from which point the smacks usually took their departure. Trips averaged 12 days, during which a haul of about 10,000 oysters could generally be expected. Some queer things happened to smacks in this fishery, almost as though the sea was more than usually reluctant to yield its harvest. One fine winter's morning in 1900 found the powerful Brightlingsea ketch smack *Emma* running east-wards across the North Sea before a light breeze, bound for Terschelling. The log had spun off 60 miles since it was streamed off the Suffolk coast, and skipper Bob Crickmar hummed a tune at the tiller, while the crew prepared gear; suddenly with no warning from the placid sea a huge freak wave rose up astern and broke aboard her. Tons of water smashed down along her deck, badly injuring all the crew except one apprentice. The dinghy lay shattered in its gripes and the hatches were gone, leaving her half full of water. Painfully the crew pumped her out and, under their direction, the boy brought the wreck on the wind; but it took two days and nights to beat slowly back to the Essex coast, and by that time the men, many with broken limbs, were almost exhausted, and the boy was little better. That night as he nodded at the tiller she gently grounded on the Shipwash sand, where the Harwich lifeboat found her and towed them in. *Emma* was one of the last smacks to work at Terschelling.

Many of these Essex smacks were used at times in "salvaging", that is rendering assistance to and rescuing the crews and passengers from the

38

tremendous numbers of ships wrecked off the coasts of Essex and Suffolk in the maze of shoals and channels. If the vessel could not be got off
they would salvage gear, sails, spars, equipment, fittings and any of the
cargo, if it was valuable. All this was often done in bad weather and at
great risk but much money could be made at times and my great-grandfather Tom Barnard and his sons and his smacks were leading partici-
pants. There is no evidence that the *Pioneer* ever engaged in this work,
which was much more profitable than fishing, if opportunity offered, just
as was acting as unlicensed pilots to ships whose masters became confused
in navigating this dangerous coast, usually in bad weather or fog.

Apart from the activities already described, some Essex smacks were
employed on contract for £12 a week as fish carriers for the great fleets of
lumbering Grimsby, Hull, Yarmouth and Lowestoft ketches which spent
the year round trawling the Dogger bank. They were ideal for this work,
being fast and capable of driving through the foulest weather, and, blow
high or low, they usually got to Barking or Billingsgate before the cargo
turned. Colne smacks were also employed in the seasonal carrying of
fresh salmon from the western Irish ports of Sligo and Westport, on the

coast of County Mayo, round the northern tip of Ireland to the Liverpool market. This was perhaps the hardest trade of all, for the coast is exposed to the full sweep and fury of the North Atlantic, and most smacks took the precaution of reeving chain reef pendants to stand the hard driving. They usually made the round voyage to Liverpool and back in four days, no mean feat in such small vessels. They must have been stirring sights, cracking on and plunging bowsprit in the seaway off Malin Head or the Bloody Foreland, with the precious freight of 100 boxes full of fresh salmon checked off in the hold. The Rowhedge *New Unity* was one of several Colne smacks engaged at times in the equally unrecorded and arduous voyages to the German and other Baltic ports with barrelled herring shipped from Stornaway.

In fact there was nothing these men wouldn't or couldn't tackle to get a living when the fishing was dull. One of them, the Rowhedge *Young Pheasant*, owned by Sam Mills, even became an early torpedo boat! During the 1870s the Whitehead company was experimenting with the first propelled torpedoes, and selected the Wallet as a suitable trials area for the new weapon. A local craft was required for the experiments and Sam Mills got the job, the *Young Pheasant* being fitted with a form of dropping gear (tubes had not then been perfected) and for several months she presented the unique sight of a sailing smack carrying a torpedo.

Some smacks were in the cattle trade from the Channel Islands to Weymouth at certain times of the year. The Brightlingsea *Globe* was typical, being licenced to carry 19 swine in the hold and two cows on deck. The poor beasts must have suffered in the race off Alderney, especially the cows, for it was the boy's job to truss up the boom to clear their backs when going about. However, conditions in that trade were easy compared with those existing aboard the Mersea smack *Essex*, which in 1839 discharged a cargo of no less than 41 Norwegian ponies on Brightlingsea hard for auction.

The Rowhedge *Aquiline* and *New Blossom*, Charles Crosby's 33-ton ketch, were often employed in the French spring potato trade from St Malo and St Michael's to Colchester, shipments being made for Baxter and Co. *New Blossom* also often shipped the village's coal from Shields and frequently voyaged to the Baltic with cargoes of coal or barrelled herring prior to the 1880s. When Wivenhoe dry dock was built in the early nineties, *Aquiline's* owner contracted to supply all the shingle needed for the cement, and all this was dug by hand from Colne beach, sailed upstream, and discharged by hand, 22 tons per trip – and it needed several hundred tons to complete the job. *Aquiline* and her sisters were no strangers to the London river either. Apart from landing fish at Billingsgate and Gravesend, they often sailed up to Deadman's Creek, Rotherhithe, to load imported oysters from the Tagus, Brittany or Chesapeake Bay, sailing home to lay them, usually at West Mersea in the extensive layings then owned by the Heaths of Wivenhoe.

But the dredging of oysters and scallops in deeper waters was the main work of the *Pioneer* and her contemporaries. In 1874 she was sailing from Brightlingsea under the managing ownership of Brightlingsea butcher Joseph Alexander. She seems still to have then been rigged as a cutter but during the 1880s a series of severe gales caused the loss of many similar smacks and owners began to think of larger vessels. The desire for greater length brought a change to ketch rig, to maintain the smallest number of crew. In 1889 the *Pioneer*'s owners decided to have her lengthened by 11ft amidships to increase capacity. At the same time a wet well was built into the new space to enable the smack to remain longer on the grounds when dredging for oysters or scallops. The catch was held in strong sacks suspended by ropes lowered into the well, which was allowed to fill with sea water entering via holes drilled through the planking in way of it on each side of the bottom.

Lengthening smacks and other craft, including some yachts, was frequently done during the nineteenth century to increase hull volume for commercial or pleasure purposes. Usually the existing hull was placed on sliding ways, carefully plumbed and well cradled. Then the decision was made as to where the hull was to be cut through transversely, usually at the point of greatest breadth and fullness of section, though these were not always coincidental. Then shipwrights got to work with sharp, crosscut two-handed saws and cut through the hull, including the keel and the other main longitudinal members. The two parts were then struck apart by drawing one away from the other for the desired distance, plumbing and alignment being carefully preserved. The new length of the keel was then scarphed and bolted to the ends of the existing keel and new pieces of keelson and beam shelf were fitted to the old by scarphing and bolting. The two parts of the existing hull would hold their shape well but it was usually necessary to increase the beam, not just in a fair line between the two but rather more, to retain power to carry the greater sail area of the lengthened smack. This appears to have been done to the *Pioneer* whose remeasured breadth was 15ft 2in against the original 13ft 11in. They must have allowed the sheer batten to flow more fully and to have adjusted the heads of the frames close to the cut accordingly. New frames and floors were fitted to suit the shape achieved with fairing ribbands in the amidship part and the whole work faired to the existing ends. New amidships planking was fitted and a shift of butts arranged into the

41

planking at the ends. The additional deck beams and new hatches were fitted and new deck planking laid over the increased length, with a suitable shift of butts into the old.

The wet well had a truncated, pyramid shaped access trunk from the deck with a strong wooden grating over its top. The top of the well, about 3ft below the deck, was level across the hull in the *Pioneer*. What is unusual about her lengthening is that the frames in way of it are very widely spaced, which is a weak feature of the structure after lengthening, though the hull remained in fishing use into the 1920s and was afloat into the 1940s.

In the later years of the 19th century yachting rivalled and then eclipsed the Essex sea fisheries. The smaller 12- and 18-tonners became popular for working the Thames estuary and its approaches as these could be more economically laid up all summer while their crews made more colourful pages of sailing history and much more money as captains and crews of yachts. The days of the big smacks were numbered, though as late as 1890 Brightlingsea had a fleet of 52. Twelve years later several poisoning scares killed the demand for sea oysters and the remaining smacks took to working down Channel from January to March, usually dredging scallops and oysters from the French ports, notably Boulogne, and sending the catch to London by the night steamer. Shoreham and Newhaven were also used when dredging the extensive grounds off Beachy Head in company with some very fine smacks from Emsworth, Hampshire. About 1910 extreme weather conditions kept a dozen Brightlingsea boats in port there for seven weeks as the dredges could not be kept on the ground in the terrific seas running. All that time the crews earned nothing and ended in debt for their food.

The First World War dealt a great blow to the big Essex smacks and, though fish prices were high, several were sold away to Lowestoft and elsewhere while others were working on Government fishing contracts, mainly stowboating. After the war a few carried on in the traditional ways, supplemented by a few old Lowestoft steam drifters, though with the exception of these and four or five paddle dredgers owned by the Colne and the Burnham oyster fisheries, steam found no place in the Essex fleet.

The *Pioneer* continued to sail from Brightlingsea and by 1919 Joseph Eagle, one of an old local fishing family was managing owner. The trade slumps of the early 1920s brought further change of ownership and eventually she was laid up and became a houseboat at East Mersea, later being towed round to West Mersea, on the nearby river Blackwater, where she was moored on the mud. After harsh winters and hot summers the

Pioneer lost caulking and began to fill each tide. Eventually she subsided into the mud with little to show her end. By 1998 few remembered the *Pioneer*, but interest in restoring various Essex smacks led to a decision to have the last of the bigger smacks restored and so the *Pioneer* was raised from her grave, something which would have truly astonished her original owners and crews, though I very much doubt they would applaud revival of a type of craft which to them meant often very hard and ill rewarded work, frequently in bad conditions.

On 3 December 1998, in a bitter wind, the hulk of the *Pioneer* was raised and was floated to Mersea hard, to await transport by road to her place of rebuilding, several miles inland. There she was carefully cleaned, blocked up, shored and plumbed – with the many structural members also recovered with her put in place so that an accurate restoration could begin by Brian Kennell and Shaun White. Both are experienced in the rebuilding, in some instances amounting to new building of smacks and the rebirth of the *Pioneer* is their biggest job to date. When completed she will sail again, rigged as a ketch, to become a symbol of Essex and a reminder of the long maritime traditions and skills of our county.

Pioneer in the Strood Channel at West Mersea, she lay here from 1942 to 1998.

43

OFFICIAL NUMBER OF SHIP _48.991_

Number, Year, and Port of Registry	_1_/_1889_ _Colchester_	Number, Year, and Port of previous Registry (if any).	_1_/_1865_ _Colchester_	British or Foreign-built	_British_

PARTICULARS OF TONNAGE.

GROSS TONNAGE.		In Register Tons	In Cubic Metres	DEDUCTIONS ALLOWED.	In Register Tons	In Cubic M...
Under Tonnage Deck		32.18		On account of Space required for Propelling Power		
Closed-in Spaces above the Tonnage Deck (if any)				On account of Spaces occupied by Seamen or Apprentices, and appropriated to their use, and kept free from Goods or Stores of every kind, not being the personal property of the Crew. These Spaces are the following, viz.:—		
Space or Spaces between Decks						
Poop						
Forecastle						
Roundhouse						
Other Closed-in Spaces (if any), as follows:				_Deduction under Sec 79 M.S.A. 1894, and Sec 54 M.S.A 1906 as follows_		
				Boiler Space · 1.60 Tons.		
				Boatswain Store · 3.00 —·—	5.40	15.28
				Sail Room .80 —·—		
GROSS TONNAGE		32.18	41.07			
DEDUCTIONS, as per Contra		5.40	15.28			
Register Tonnage		~~32.18~~ 26.78	~~41.07~~ 45.79	TOTAL DEDUCTIONS	5.40	15.2

Names, Residence, and Description of the Owners, and Number of Sixty-four Shares held by each Owner	_Joseph Alexander of Brightlingsea in the County of Essex. Bu..._

Dated _20" Febry 1889_

Col. 1.	Col. 2.	Col. 3.	Col. 4.	Col. 5.	Col. 6.	Col. 7.
Number of Transaction	Letter denoting Mortgages, and Certificates of Mortgage.	Name of Person from whom Title is derived.	Number of Shares affected	Date of Registry.	Nature and Date of Transaction.	Name, Residence, and Occupation of Transferee, Mortgagee, or other Person acquiring Title or Power.
1	A	Joseph Alexander	64	3" April 1889 10 A.M.	Mortgage A) dated 27th March 1889 for £300 and interest at 5%	Robert Aldous of Brightlingsea in the County of Essex Ship Builder.
2	A	Robert Aldous	64	8th March 1911 P.M.V.	Died 25th October 1910. Will dated 25th August 1910 appointing Albert James Aldous Executor. Probate granted in His Majesty's Probate Court London on the 26th January 1911.	Albert James Ald... of Brightlings... in the county of E... - Ship. Builder.
3	A	Robert Aldous	64	23rd April 1912. am 10.	Died 25th October 1910. Will dated 25th August 1910 appointing Eliza Aldous, Albert James Aldous, Frank Disney Sisting and Hazel Polley, Executors to whom Probate was granted in the Principal Probate Registry of the High Court of Justice on the 26th January 1911.	Eliza Aldous of 42 High Brightlingsea. Widow. Frank Disney Sisting of Thorington Hall, ... ington - Farmer. Hazel Polley of 63 Chapel Rd Brightlingsea - Boa... Builder - all in the... of Essex - together wi... Albert James Aldous already recorded by... transmission N.S G... ...Kett. Registra...
4	A	Eliza Aldous, Albert James Aldous, Frank Disney Sisting and Hazel Polley - joint mortgagees	64	3rd Octr 1912 am 10.	Bill of sale under mortgage A dated 1st October 1912	Albert Charles Bentley of 62 North Str, Colche... in the county of Essex - Solicitors clerk -
5		Albert Charles Bentley	64	3rd Octr 1912 am 10	Bill of sale dated 2nd October 1912	Albert James Aldous of 9 Tower Street, Brig... lingsea in the county of Essex - Ship Builde... ...Kett. Registrar

NAME OF SHIP *Pioneer*

Whether a Sailing or Steam Ship; if Steam, how propelled.	*Sailing*	Where built *East Donyland County of Essex*	When built *1864* Lengthened *1889*	Name of Builder *Peter Harris East Donyland*

			Feet.	Tenths.
Number of Decks	*One*	Length from Forepart of Stem under the Bowsprit to the Aft side of the Head of the Stern-post	*64*	*-*
Number of Masts	*Two*	Main Breadth to Outside of Plank	*15*	*2*
Rigged	*Ketch*	Depth in Hold from Tonnage Deck to Ceiling at Midships	*6*	*9*
Stern	*Square*	Depth in Hold from Upper Deck to Ceiling at Midships in the case of Ships of Three Decks and upwards		
Build	*Carvel*	Length of Engine Room (if any)		
Galleries	*none*			
Head	*none*			
Framework	*Wood*			

PARTICULARS OF ENGINES (if any).

No. of Engines.	Description.	Whether British or Foreign made.	When made.	Name and Address of Maker.	Diameter of Cylinders.	Length of Stroke.	Number of Horses Power (combined).

Sixty four 64

(Signed) *H. de Mornelfied* Registrar.

Col. 8.	Col. 9.	Col. 10.	Col. 11.	Col. 12.	Col. 13.	Col. 14.
Number and Account of subsequent Transaction, showing how Interest disposed of.	Number of Transaction under which Title acquired.	Names of Owners.	Mortgages and Certificates of Mortgage.	Names of Mortgagees or Attorneys under Certificates of Mortgage.	Number of Shares.	REMARKS.
	1	Joseph Alexander	Mortgage (A) for £300 & int at 5%	Robert Aldous	64	Joseph Alexander of Brightlingsea designated Managing Owner. Advice under his hand received 20 Feb 1889 H de Mornelfied
			Total 3 April 1889 H de Mornelfied R		64	
From 19a Decd 8/12	0/2	Joseph Alexander	Mortgage (A) for £200 and interest at 5%	Albert James Aldous	64	
			Total 8th March 1912		64	
	0/3	Joseph Alexander	Mortgage (A) for £300 and interest at 5%	E. Aldous A. J. Aldous J. D. Girling H. Polley joint Mortgagees	64	
			Total 23rd April 1912		64	
	5	A. J. Aldous	Total 3rd October 1912		64	Albert James Aldous of No 9 Tower Street, Brightlingsea, Essex designated Managing owner. Advice under his hand received this 3rd October 1912. H Wett Regr
		See Folio 154			64	

To Folio No 154

Port Number and Year ____1889____   *From Folio No 3*

Official Number ____48991.____   Gross 32.18

Name of Ship ____Pioneer____   ~~Regd 32.18~~   **TRANSACTIONS subsequent to**

26.48 (See Folio 3)

Col. 1.	Col. 2.	Col. 3.	Col. 4.	Col. 5.	Col. 6.	Col. 7.
Number of Transaction.	Letter denoting Mortgages, and Certificates of Mortgage.	Name of Person from whom Title is derived.	Number of Shares affected.	Date of Registry.	Nature and Date of Transaction.	Name, Residence, and Occupation of Transferee, Mortgagee, or other Person acquiring Title or Power.
6		Albert James Aldous.	64.	24th Decr 1912 noon	Bill of Sale dated 24th December 1912.	Erney John Beer of No 10 Eastern Ro Brightlingsea in the county of Essex Mariner. *Skett. Regist*
7		Erney John Beer	64	25th Sepr 1916 am.10.	Bill of Sale dated 5th September 1916.	Albert James Ald of 52 Church Roa Brightlingsea in county of Essex — Shipowner *Skett. Regist*
8		Albert James Aldous	64	2nd July 1918 am.10	Bill of Sale dated 5th February 1918	Joseph Martin Eag of 15 Queen Street, Brightlingsea, in county of Essex — oyster merchant *Skett. Reg*
9		Joseph Martin Eagle	64	9th February 1921 pm. 2.30	Bill of Sale dated 12th January 1920	Thomas Edward Poole of 49 Colne Road, Brightl in the county of Essex — ship owner. *F Hadler*

Certificate cancelled and Registry closed.
29th November 1929, on Registry Anew at Colchester
in consequence of alterations in means of
propulsion

         W Brightmore Registrar

First Registry—*continued.*

Col. 8. Number and account of subsequent Transaction, showing how Interest disposed of.	Col. 9. Number of Transaction under which Title acquired.	Col. 10. Names of Owners.	Col. 11. Mortgages and Certificates of Mortgage.	Col. 12. Names of Mortgagees and Attorneys under Certificates of Mortgage.	Col. 13. Number of Shares.	Col. 14. REMARKS.
	6	E. J. Beere	Total 24th Dec: 1912		64 64	Sydney John Beere of No. 10. Eastern Road, Brightlingsea. Essex, designated Managing owner. Advice under his hand received this 24th Dec: 1912. Skett. Regr.
	7	A. J. Aldous	Total. 25th Sep: 1916.		64 64	Albert James Aldous of No. 52 Church Road, Brightlingsea. Essex, designated Managing owner. Advice under his hand received this 25th September 1916. Skett. Regr.
	8	J. M. Eagle	Total 2nd July 1918		64 64	Joseph Martin Eagle, of 15 Queen Street, Brightlingsea, Essex designated Managing owner. Advice under his hand received this 2nd July, 1918 Skett Regr
	9	T. E. Poole	Total 9th Feby. 1921.		64 64	Thomas Edward Poole, of 49 Sherfield, Brightlingsea, Essex, designated Managing owner. Advice received under his hand dated this 9th Feby. 1921 J. Parker Actg Regr.

OWNERS OF PIONEER

1865   **CHARLES FORD BISHOP**
Master Mariner
Cowes, Isle of White
Lloyds Agent office at:
2 Tudor House
Bath Road, Cowes
Home, The Lawn
Worsley Road, Gurnard

1866   **THOMAS BRASSEY**
Gentleman.
Beauport, Sussex
Son of Thomas Brassey I, world famous railway contractor. On July 15, 1876, he set sail with his wife Annie, their four children, and two pugs, for a cruise around the world. Thomas was an enthusiastic sailor – his steam yacht, the "Sunbeam", built at Seacombe in 1874, was 157 feet long and carried a crew of 30. Thomas became secretary to the admiralty, received a knighthood in 1881, became Baron Brassey of Bulkeley in 1886 and Earl Brassey in 1911. Among other appointments, he also was made Governor of Victoria, Australia and Lord Warden of the Cinque Ports.

1868   **JOSEPH ALEXANDER**
Butcher and Publican
Resident of The Ship Inn,
9 Victoria Place
Brightlingsea

THOMAS BRASSEY (II)
at helm of the Sunbeam

ROBERT ALDOUS
re-rigged Pioneer to ketch, lengthened 53ft to 64ft, had well fitted in 1889. Provided mortgage at the same time for £300, interest at 5%

1912   ERNEST JOHN BEERE
        Mariner
        10 Eastern Road
        Brightlingsea.
        Shipowner

1916   ALBERT JAMES ALDOUS
        Ship Owner & Oyster Merchant
        52 *Church Road*
        Brightlingsea

1918   JOSEPH MARTIN EAGLE
        Oyster merchant
        15 Queens Street
        Brightlingsea

ERNEY BEERE
owner 1912 - 1916 and
skipper in 1909 and 1926

left: Joseph & Noble Eagle
outside store on the Hard.

below: JOSEPH EAGLE
c.1920

above: THOMAS POOLE, *centre in bowler hat, with Colne River Police*

1921   THOMAS EDWARD POOLE
Ship Owner and Inspector
of the Colne River Police
49 Colne Road
Brightlingsea
Lost sails and rigging after a fire
in 1929.

1938   GEORGE DREWELL
Club Steward
East Mersea Golf Club
Turned Pioneer *into a houseboat*
by cutting out most of deck and
building a shed on top.

1942   HAROLD VICTOR MICHELL
Firs Road, West Mersea
Pioneer *sank soon after being*
towed from East to West Mersea.

VIC MICHELL *owned* Pioneer
at West Mersea in 1942

KNOWN MASTERS OF PIONEER

Standing on left: JOSEPH RUFFLE, *skipper 1904, grandfather of Keith Ruffle who has helped with the blacksmithing during the restoration.*

1865	William Sansom		1923	Charles Munson
1867	Isaiah Powell		1924	Arthur French
1868	John Foot		1926	Ernest Beere
1881	George Butcher		1926	Charles Munson
1887	Mr Lamb			
1904	Joseph Ruffle			
1905	William Steward			
1906	William White			
1906	Harry Chaplin			
1907	Charles Munson			
1907	Arthur Oliver			
1907	John Handley			
1908	J. Ruffle			
1909	Ezekial Slowgrove			
1909	Ernest Beere			
1922	Ernest Baker			

WILLIAM WHITE
skipper of Pioneer *1906 Great-grandfather to Shaun White, restoration shipwright*

51

Form No. 11.

SAILING SHIP.

MORTGAGE (to se

(handwritten margin, left side, vertical): William Howe Colchester 25 May 1868 ... 1 P.M. Registrar ... Entd. 1 P.M ... no ...

Official Number of Ship *48,991*

| Port Number...... *One* | Port of Registry...... *Colchester* | British or |

Build - - - *Carvel*

Galleries - - - *None*

Head - - - *None*

Framework - - - *Wood*

Number of Decks - *One*

Number of Masts - *One*

Rigged - - - *Smack*

Stern - - - *Square*

MEASUREMENTS.

Length from the fore part of Stem under the Bo
to the aft side of the head of the stern-post -

Main breadth to outside plank - - -

Depth in hold from Tonnage Deck to Ceili
Midships - - - - - - -

(ᵃ) "I" or "we."

(ᵇ) "Me" or "us."

(ᶜ) "Myself" or "our-selves."

(ᵈ) "My" or "our."

(ᵉ) "I am" or "we are."

(f) Insert the day fixed for payment of principal as above.

(g) If any prior incum-brance add, "save as ap-"pears by the Registry "of the said Ship."

(ᵃ) *I* the undersigned *Joseph Alexander of Brightlingse*

in consideration of *One hundred and fifty pounds Sterl.* this day lent to (ᵇ)

do hereby for (ᶜ) *myself* and (ᵈ) *my* heirs, covenant with the said *George bra*

executors, or administrators will pay to the said *George bracknell his executors ho*

together with interest thereon at the rate of *Ten pounds* per cent. per annum on the *1*

day (ᵃ) *I* or (ᵈ) *my* heirs, executors, or administrators, will, during such time as the

interest on the whole or such part thereof as may for the time being remain unpaid, at the rate

and *thirtieth* day of *April* in every year; and for better securing to the

the repayment in manner aforesaid of the said principal sum and interest (ᵃ) *I* hereby m

Sixty four sixty fourth shares, of which (ᵉ) *I am* the Owner in the Ship above part

is made on condition that the power of sale which by the Merchant Shipping Act, 1854, is ves

shall not be exercised until the said (f) *thirtieth* day of *October* . Lastly, (ᵉ) *I* f

and *his* assigns that (ᵃ) *I* have power to mortgage in manner aforesaid the above-menti

and administrator all my interest in a certain blacy in the Brightlingsea

to use my name and act as my attorney

In witness whereof (ᵃ) *I* have hereto subscribed (ᵈ) *my* name and affixed (ᵈ)

Executed by the above-named *Joseph Alexander*

in the presence of *Ellis C Attwood*

Brightlingsea

9041.—5 rms.—2/64.   EYRE & SPOTTISWOODE, Her Majesty's Printers.

incipal Sum and Interest).

Name of Ship *Pioneer*

| *British* | Where built...... {*at East Donyland in the County of Essex*} | When built...... {*On the 22nd day of December 1864*} |

Feet.	Tenths.	TONNAGE.	No. of Tons.
		Tonnage under Tonnage Deck - - - -	23 · 18
53	"	Closed-in spaces above the Tonnage Deck, if any; viz.:	
13	9	Space or spaces between Decks - - - -	
		Poop - - - - - - -	
6	9	Round-house - - - - -	
		Other inclosed spaces, if any, naming them - -	
		Total Register Tonnage - -	*18?*

County of Essex Butcher and Publican

George Bracknell of Lowestoft in the County of ~~Essex~~ Suffolk Engineer firstly: That (a) *I* or (d) *my* heirs, *Executors Administrators and Assigns* the said sum of *One hundred and fifty pounds* *tors and assigns* day of *October* next; and secondly, that if the said principal sum is not paid on the said rt thereof remain unpaid, pay to the said *George Bracknell* *and* per cent. per annum, by equal half-yearly payments on the *thirtieth* day of *October* *e Bracknell* said *George Bracknell* l, and in her boats, guns, ammunition, small arms, and appurtenances. (a) *I* declare that this mortgage *George Bracknell* *and* (d) *my* heirs, covenant with the said *George Bracknell* that the same are free from incumbrances (e) *And I assign unto the said George Bracknell his Executor* *ance society whereby the said ship is insured for loss with full power for the said George Bracknell* his *thirtieth* day of *April* One thousand eight hundred and *sixtyeight*.

Joseph Alexander

02.

PIONEER, THE STORY SO FAR

By Brian Kennell

Early in June 1998 on a hot, sunny day, someone on the waterfront in West Mersea may have spotted three figures plodding through knee-deep mud towards some weedy remnants poking out of the mud. I think this moment marked the start of a remarkable endeavour to raise the remains of the most complete example of a Brightlingsea Skillinger that survives.

The story begins the previous year when John Milgate of Peldon and a band of volunteers dug the smack *ABC* out of the Feldy Marsh opposite West Mersea. Although she had been sunk since the Second World War, there was a substantial amount of the boat left. Certainly enough for an experienced boatbuilder to be able to reconstruct her. This set my colleague Shaun White and me thinking about other wrecks of smacks. We were looking for boats in the 30 to 35ft long range as we thought it would be easier to find potential clients for small smacks than larger boats. As boatbuilders involved in the restoration of a number of smacks in recent years, we thought it might be a good idea to have one or two restorable wrecks tucked up our sleeve.

The first boat we actually surveyed was the *William and Eliza*, known locally as the *Tally*. She lies opposite Brightlingsea, buried in the mud. An interesting boat, she was built in Tollesbury in 1856 and had a lute stern. She was owned by two brothers, "The Tally Boys", well known for their eccentricity. A friend of ours, Rupert Marks, for whom we had recently rebuilt a smack, said he would like to come too. So on a cold spring day in 1998 we headed off to examine her remains. We found that although most of the boat above the mud was heavily decayed, probing the mud inside the hull revealed that part to be complete. Afterwards, as we chatted over a warming cup of tea at Shaun's house, we agreed that it was perfectly feasible to dig her out but she might be a little bit big at 40ft from stem to stern. Shaun then produced a photograph of his wife's grandfathers smack, the *Vanduara* CK26. She was a handsome ketch with a sweeping sheer and a long bowsprit and she was big. Originally she was cutter rigged when built in 1880. She was built by R. Aldous and must have been one of the largest cutters built on the Colne at 67ft overall. Her boom would have been about 50ft long, which must have been a nightmare to handle in a North Sea gale, (maybe they used a trysail?). At any rate she was converted to the more convenient ketch rig in 1897. Now I knew that many big smacks had worked out of the river Colne in the last

century, and I was vaguely aware that the remnants of afew of them were still around, but I was surprised to learn from Shaun that the bones of the *Vanduara* were still to be seen.

A couple of months later in May we sailed down the Blackwater and into the Colne on Rupert's smack *Hyacinth*. We were in search of big smacks. Sometime in the previous two months a strange transformation had taken place. No longer were we looking for handy sized small smacks, we were looking for huge boats, anything up to 80ft long. Quite what we intended to do once we had found one did not seem clear to me, but Shaun and Rupert seemed to be filled with a missionary's zeal, so I kept quiet.

Shaun had already done some preliminary explorations and we were going to look at the wrecks of three boats up the Pyefleet channel. One of the smacks was a large Jersey built boat called *Heiress*. The other two were Colchester boats, the *Guide* and, of course, the *Vanduara*, and all three had wet wells. Unfortunately, although we had an interesting hour or so in the mud and we found afew artefacts, whichever way we looked at the *Guide* and *Vanduara* there was not enough of either to warrant digging them out of the mud. I said, "We might as well go and look at *Pioneer* in Mersea, there's more of her left than these two put together". Which brings us back to our trip to Mersea in early June.

55

Twenty-five years ago, when I was a boy with a lugsail dinghy I sailed around the bow of the *Pioneer*. It stood high above the water, the windlass and a little of foredeck still in place. Now, as we walked up the mud I saw that the bow had completely collapsed, a victim of the '87 hurricane we were told. As we got closer we could see the decking on top of the wet well, proof for us that we were looking at a large Colchester smack. *Pioneer* was far more intact than the other wrecks we had examined. She had a 30ft section in the centre of the boat that was complete up to the beamshelf. Soundings in the mud showed that the counter stern was missing, but the rest of her was there, deep in the mud. In Pyefleet the wet well bulkheads were standing above the mud, the top of *Pioneer's* wet well was flush with the mud.

Pioneer was not built with a wet well. She was built in 1864 for Charles Bishop a Master Mariner from the Isle Of Wight and was the first boat registered on the Mercantile Navy List in 1865. This was a period of great smack building activity on the Colne, dozens of boats the size of *Pioneer* were coming off the ways in Brightlingsea, Rowhedge and Wivenhoe. In Edward Dickin's History of Brightlingsea he records that there were about 200 Colchester smacks between 15 and 40 tons in 1861. Charles Bishop had another smack built afew months after *Pioneer*, the *Albatross*. It seems likely that smack owning on the Colne was not as profitable as he thought since he sold *Pioneer* within a couple of years. *Pioneer* was 53ft from stem to sternpost, cutter rigged, registered as built in East Donyland by Peter Harris of Rowhedge. Her fishing number was CK18. In 1888 she is marked in the register as broken up but she reappears in the 1889 register as lengthened to 64ft bp and altered to ketch rig. Overall her length would have been increased to around 70ft Her beam increased by about a foot to 15ft and 2 tenths and her depth of hold remained at 6ft and 9 tenths. She would have had a draught of between 8 and 9ft This is when the wet well was installed, this type of work being common in the 1880s and many smacks had the same treatment. Robert Aldous of Brightlingsea lengthened *Pioneer*. Smacks the size of *Pioneer* worked all around the British Isles and North Sea dredging oysters and the addition of a wet well increased the time she could keep her catch alive and consequently increased her range.

We started planning our next move. There was now no doubt that we were going to try and raise the remains, but how? She was buried 9ft deep in the mud at the stern and the bow had nearly disappeared. She had been lying there since 1942, towed from East Mersea to West Mersea by Bob Stoker, a local fisherman. Bob, now in his eighties, remembers there being a lot of paperwork involved due to the war. He towed her with his own

smack the *Priscilla*. Unfortunately soon after she was moored close to the saltings above the Old City, she broke her moorings in a gale and sank. The deck had been cut out and the steward of East Mersea Golf Club had started to build a shed to turn her into a houseboat, presumably stopped by the war. The shed had washed off in the 1953 floods. Local boatbuilder Dick Gladwell remembers pulling up the floorboards to re-use when he was a youngster. As a boy, fisherman Bill Read thought that if he and his mates could only block up the hole in the port quarter they could get her to float again. Now she was full of junk, the largest item was a Merlin aero engine, dumped there by a local fisherman, the most inexplicable a lawnmower.

The obvious way to move the hundreds of tons of mud in and around *Pioneer* was with a high pressure hose and fortunately we knew someone who had a pontoon and firepump. Once the mud was cleared the wreck had to be made to float. Airbags were the only way that we could think of to achieve this because the lack of water over the wreck at high water meant that the buoyancy had to be low inside the boat or strapped under the turn of the bilge. Having floated our wreck, what did we do with it then? Somehow it had to be placed in a position suitable for craning onto road transport for the journey to Rupert's barn in Great Totham some 10 miles away.

This work would not be cheap, but fortunately Rupert agreed to underwrite the expenses involved in retrieving the wreck. With this sort of backing we set to work with a will, organising the various experts we needed to ensure success. Another milestone that we passed was in late September when the naval architect David Cannell came to value *Pioneer*. This was necessary because we had been unable to conclusively establish who owned her. David drew the obvious conclusion that she was valueless, and impressed us immensely by not telling us that we were insane, although I privately still had misgivings about the feasibility of the whole thing. A tremendous stroke of good fortune came when I contacted John Wise of JW Automarine about airbags. Not only did John volunteer to come and advise us when we were ready to lift the *Pioneer*, but he also arranged free use of the bags, saving us around £1000 worth of hire fees. Tidetables were studied and dates were set and discarded to make a start. It was quite important to get it right as we were attempting the job late in the year and daylight was at a premium. Finally a date was set for my colleague from Maldon, Ged Wright, to tow his pontoon and firepump down to Mersea. In the days leading up to the start Shaun and I busied ourselves preparing equipment and tools. It is very difficult to do this when you are attempting something so out of the ordinary. We reckoned that one of our greatest problems would be moving around in knee-deep mud, so we made three mudskids, which proved very successful.

I think the moment that I became hopelessly ensnared by the project was when I read an account of a voyage by another big smack, the *Excellent*, CK30. The article appeared in the *Brightlingsea Parish Magazine*, the vicar at the time was Arthur Pertwee, who had a special interest in the sea. He actually sailed on several long voyages on big smacks, sharing the cramped reality of life at sea with the crew. *Excellent* was built as a ketch by Robert Aldous in 1883. Registered 39 tons, she would have been about 70ft long. In 1887 Aldous had added a wet well. Written by one of the crew in 1895 the article brought home the privations and risks run to bring the humble oyster home for working class tables from the Tershelling Bank. A normal trip would be about three weeks long. When they got to the grounds off the north Dutch coast, the crew of six would work for a week or more hauling the dredges. These dredges were 6ft across the blade and 7ft high and they would have worked six of them, towing on up to 90 fathoms of two inch rope. *Excellent*, like *Pioneer*, would have been fitted with two vertical hand capstans, one forward and one amidships. These winches would have been worked almost non-stop when they were fishing. This fishery off Tershelling finished before the turn of the century, due to a poisoning scare about shellfish, and the dangers that the fishermen faced in mid-winter off the north Dutch coast. In one fierce gale on the 7th March 1883 three smacks, the *Recruit*, *Mascotte* and *Conquest* were lost. I have seen the entry in the Colchester Port register for the *Mascotte* with its final bleak entry, "Missing for two months, presumed lost". The following year another gale took the *Pride* and *William & Henry* and the big smacks that remained tried other less dangerous fisheries. Most common of those were the scallop beds down Channel. An alternative to fishing was to carry cargo and many smacks worked around the British Isles when fish were scarce. The *Vanduara* is reputed to have carried stone from Wales to repair Brightlingsea Church tower. According to the port register for Colchester the vast majority of *Pioneer's* sisters were already at the end of their working lives; those that had not been lost or sold away are frequently marked in the Colchester port registry as broken up or unseaworthy in the 1890s.

At 4 o'clock in the morning on Tuesday 10th November 1998 I staggered out of bed to join Ged on his fishing boat at the yard in Maldon. Not only were we towing his pontoon, we were towing Rupert's 12ft dinghy and a large aluminium dory that had been kindly loaned to us. We had a cold but uneventful trip down the river and as dawn broke we were met by local oyster merchant Alan Bird, who was helping us to position the pontoon so as not to damage adjacent oyster layings. Rupert and Shaun soon arrived and we set-to cutting a channel through the mud from the low water mark up to the wreck. This channel was to wash away the spoil from around *Pioneer*. The channel needed to be at least 4ft deep by the time we got up to the *Pioneer*. This would enable us to wash the mud out below the turn of the bilge, thus giving us a better chance of breaking her grip of the mud with the air-bags. By mid-afternoon we had reached the boat but had failed to get the channel deep enough. We had hired a slurry pump to clear the inside of the hull, so we figured that we may be able to use the pump outside the hull to clear the wallow. If we couldn't, it would add at least a week to the schedule – time we could ill afford.

By Wednesday afternoon we had cleared as much mud as we could without the slurry pump; the Merlin engine and the windlass were also starting to loom large. Alan Bird came to the rescue and lifted both out with his mooring launch and put them on Wyatts hard. The windlass was to be taken up to Rupert's barn along with some framing we had removed from the port quarter, but the engine was a problem. After some discussion we shelved a decision on what to do with the engine and concentrated on getting the slurry pump, which must have weighed 5cwt into the dory. Again Alan saved the day, and next morning in the pre-dawn rain he lifted the pump into the dory with his launch. Within afew hours we had cleared the mud from the wet well along with a defunct fishing boat wheelhouse, complete with instruments and broken glass, and what Ged identified as a Morris Cowley engine. Meanwhile at the top of Wyatts hard they were almost fighting for the privilege of giving themselves hernias taking away the Merlin engine, which proves that we were not the only daft ones in Mersea that autumn.

By now we were getting used to working in soft sticky mud. Ged dealt with his pump, sorting out the hoses every morning and actually hosing the mud most of the time. Rupert, Shaun and I had "borrowed" dry suits from the Navy and the Customs and Excise. These suits were a godsend and without them the job would have been a lot more difficult. They enabled us to really get stuck in (literally) clearing debris, moving the hose about and retrieving useful looking bits that we wished to save. Shaun had a system for recording where in the boat loose bits of framing came from, so that later we could reassemble the upper parts of the boat that were adrift. We also had help on Thursday and Friday from my friend Richard Titchener and some moral support from my wife Sally, who visited us on several occasions.

Fortunately the slurry pump was proving it was worth its weight in gold. It easily coped with clearing the sloppy mud from around the hull, draining into a sump Ged had cut by the sternpost. The strum-box had to be regularly cleared of small bits of planking that had washed aft. All parts of the boat that had been exposed to the elements were badly eaten by gribble, but the bits buried deep in the mud were perfect. Our excavations of the wet well had shown that *Pioneer* had a very sharp deadrise and, as the mud was cleared from around the bow and stern it became apparent that she had very fine lines indeed. We were heartened by this as it would be disappointing to expend a great deal of time digging out a slow, ugly boat.

We had progressed so well in four days that we decided to give ourselves the weekend off. It also has to be said that we were completely shattered, walking around in knee-deep mud for six to seven hours a day was exhausting. John Wise was coming on Tuesday to advise us about attaching the airbags and the mud had been cleared as low as we considered practical, so we turned our minds to what we could do on Monday. Ged had suggested running a wire inside the boat from stem to stern to give us something to shackle the airbags to. Ideally the airbags would be attached to webbing straps running under the keel, but the keel was still several feet down in the mud, and it seemed unlikely we would be able to dig so deep. I had found a big coil of redundant wire in the boatyard, and a friend Jim Dines made some steel staples that we could coachscrew into the bottom of the boat for lashing the wire down to. Monday passed relatively easily threading the wire through holes we drilled by hand in the wet well bulkheads, and fixing staples down. Two strong points we used were the engine beds and steam-boiler bearers. A steam capstan had been installed in 1925 and a 35 hp engine in 1929 – interesting that a winch was considered more important than an engine. Incidentally the engine was

installed in the foc'sle with a shaft running through the wet well and out on the starboard quarter.

We met John Wise at midday on Tuesday 19th November. The tide was just leaving the *Pioneer* as we arrived. I was surprised at how philosophically John looked at our plan to raise the wreck, but after talking to him for a while I realised that he regarded *Pioneer* as an object that needed lifting rather than a boat. He thought it was important that we got strops under the keel, lifting the boat bit by bit until we had strops under her from end to end. John was not keen on our wire running through the boat, doubting the strength of our staples. It was also apparent that we would not be able to get the bags before Friday. The more we thought about it the more improbable it seemed that we could attempt a lift on the mid November set of tides. We would only have a day to fit the bags, and the working time available to us every day was getting shorter. The tides at the end of the month were higher, so a delay for 10 days could be to our advantage.

Tuesday afternoon passed grovelling at the bow, threading webbing straps under the keel ready to shackle the airbags onto. Wednesday morning was spent tidying up, unloading the slurry pump and helping Ged prepare his pontoon to tow back up to the yard at Maldon. I felt as if we were abandoning *Pioneer* to her fate once more. We all returned to our normal lives, but planned our return to Mersea.

61

Shaun and I decided to return to *Pioneer* on Saturday 28th of November. Rupert was unable to work over the weekend and Ged could not return until Sunday. We were able to clear her of mud quite easily and continued to fix staples to strong points in the bottom of the boat. It had been decided that despite John Wise's disapproval it would be impossible to attach the bags to the outside of the hull. We estimated that the aft end of the keel was still 4ft deep in the mud and we could not think of a way of getting a strop that low. On Sunday Ged arrived with the pontoon which we had loaded with the airbags. Ged moored the pontoon by the bow of the boat so we had easy access for unloading the bags. As well as Ged, Shaun and I, Richard came to help, and Andy, a friend of Rupert's. Many hands made light work and by Sunday evening not only were all the bags on, but they were partially inflated as well.

We had to be down in Mersea very early on Monday morning to inflate the bags properly before the tide came up. It was bitterly cold and I stuck close by the air compressors exhaust in the dawn, glad that it was Rupert and Shaun slithering about on top of the yellow bags blowing them up. We did not intend to move *Pioneer* until later in the week. We were not even sure we could make her float. It was quite possible that the mud which had been round her for fifty years would not readily give her up. As the tide rose we were unimpressed by its rate of flow, surely it would be a better tide by the end of the week? We judged its height against the stem and drew the conclusion that it would have to put in several feet by the end of the week for us to stand any chance of moving her out of her wallow. After another half an hour it finally dawned on us that she was afloat. Fortunately as the tide receded she sat back in her hole and we scurried about putting mooring lines out and making minor adjustments to the airbags.

Tuesday and Wednesday passed clearing up some of the gear and keeping the bags topped up, as they leaked slightly. Thursday 3rd of December was another grey, cold day, but fortunately the wind was light. Malcolm Cawdron from Mersea Marine had agreed to tow *Pioneer* to his slipway and haul her out. He and his team of men turned up an hour and a half before high water and we attached his launch to the bow. Originally we had intended to tow her out of her berth stern first down the channel we had cut, but at the last minute we had decided to drag her bow round and tow her stem first down the channel. This decision was nearly our undoing as she snagged on a fibreglass dinghy buried in the mud, and it was nearly high water before she was finally floating free. Malcolm expertly piloted his ungainly tow down through the moorings and onto the slipway cradle. This was quite a tense time as the ebb was already running and we estimated she was drawing about 9ft which was close to the available depth on the cradle. If she grounded half on and half off she would probably break up.

The winch ground into life and the remarkably fine lines of a first class Colchester smack were visible for the first time in many years. For me she is the vessel that time forgot, a throwback to a former age. The only survivor of a fleet that numbered well over a hundred in the 19th century, a type of boat that was already extinct by the 1930s. A small band of well-wishers were there to greet her emergence from the water and after a brief celebratory drink she was made safe and hauled to the top of the slip. Over the next few days we removed the airbags and washed them ready for Rupert to return them to John Wise in Norfolk. The following week Rupert, Shaun and I spent a morning levelling her up ready for the next stage, which was to survey the hull and record the lines before she was moved.

David Cannell and his assistant James Pratt, along with John Harding, a friend of Rupert's who is a surveyor, then started to measure the hull in preparation for drawing up the lines. They used high tech equipment that bounces microwaves from a fixed point onto a reflector held anywhere on the surface of the hull. The resulting data can then be fed into David Cannell's computer, which then produces a lines plan. This also has an advantage for us, the boatbuilders. Instead of having laboriously to draw out the lines of the vessel full size to be able to make patterns of every piece of wood that made up the frames, the computer can generate a pattern of the whole frame from top to bottom including the bevels. When you think that every full frame can be made up of anything up to nine separate pieces, and there are between 40 and 50 frames in *Pioneer*, the time savings possible are large.

Even after *Pioneer* was hauled out it was not clear quite what was to happen to her. If she was indeed to be rebuilt she needed to end up at Rupert's barn, but to get to the barn involved crossing two fields and that would not be possible until the summer. Leaving her on Wyatts slipway was not an option as it was expensive and they wanted their slipway for other work. Rupert finally managed to arrange with a farmer friend of his in Goldhanger for her to be blocked off in his farmyard. We had decided to use Cadman, a local crane hire company for the lift. Finding a haulage company was more difficult, several firms were contacted but they all failed to come back to us. Eventually Rupert contacted Anglia Heavy Haulage. Although they were not specifically a boat moving firm they had a large extending trailer they thought would be suitable. A date was set, Tuesday 26th of January.

LINES PLAN

LENGTH OVER ALL: 69' 11"
BEAM: 15' 2"
DRAUGHT: 7' 9"

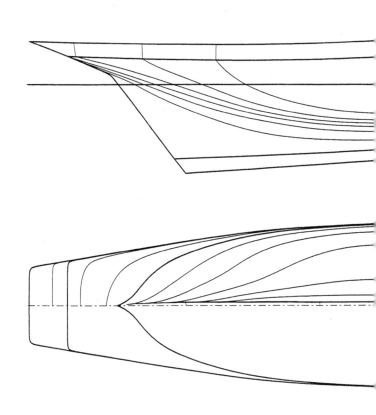

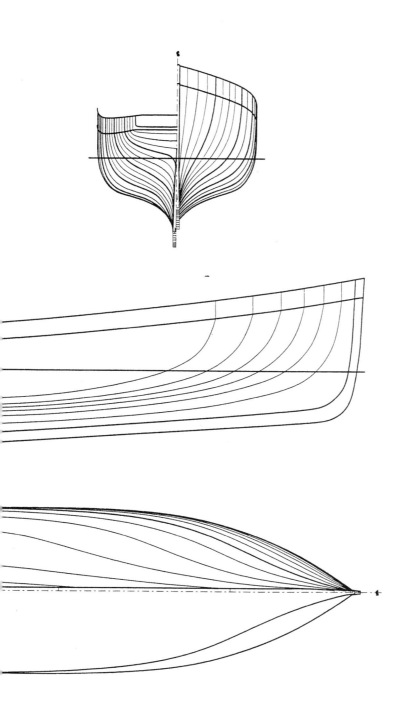

At 8 o'clock when Ged and I arrived it looked as though the whole world was there to move her. Between Cadman, Anglia Plant and Mersea Marine eight men had turned up, with Shaun, Rupert, Ged and I that made 12 in all ! We had been told by Cadman that we needed a cradle under her, as she was not strong enough to lift with two strops with spreader bars above. A cradle was going to cost £1200 so it was decided to risk it, with the help of extra spreaders to try and prevent her being crushed. The first attempt ended with the crane leg going down instead of the boat going up. Several sleepers later and the second attempt succeeded without her falling in two. The crane driver told us she weighed 21 tons as she was, a light load for the 50ft long trailer she was loaded onto.

A load as wide as *Pioneer* needed a police escort, so once the lorry had managed to manoeuvre back onto the road we waited a short while for the escort to turn up. She filled the Coast Road as we pulled off for the 10 mile journey to Goldhanger. The centre of Mersea was negotiated without incident and it was not until Peldon that we had any excitement when the sternpost clipped an electric wire and set the poles wobbling all the way down the road. Further on in Wigborough an elderly lady drove her car into the ditch to avoid us, but fortunately an AA van that happened to be following us towed her out.

Now that *Pioneer* was at Goldhanger for some months we could piece together the framing we had removed before we refloated her, especially the counter stern and stem. This would enable David Cannell to complete the lines plan and start stability calculations and a sail plan. The job of

researching her history continued, with further visits to Colchester records office and the records office in Kew. Sourcing oak bends for the framing had already begun and we were hoping to find this material in Essex or Suffolk, although the centreline and planking would have to come from further afield. We have only got as far as we have and know as much as we do because of the help we have received from other people. Many people have given us information and photographs. Others have devoted their time. We are particularly thankful for the help we have had from people in Mersea and their recollections.

For Shaun and me the *Pioneer* took on the more mundane role of a job. We had to put back in position all the framing that had either been removed from the boat during the salvage operation or had been exposed with the hose and picked up in the hope that we would be able to place it later. Early in March '99 we spent a week at the farm in Goldhanger.

Rupert had taken the remnants that were saved back to the farm, and Monday morning found us picking through an unlikely looking heap of weedy junk in the hope of finding something useful. There had been a system for marking where in the wreck we had found items, but the practical difficulties of moving around in the mud and more importantly keeping the plywood marker tags clean enough to write on had nearly defeated us. Shaun had persevered long after I had given up and now he seemed to see a pattern and value to the jumble that I could not.

One of the reasons we had set up a grid so carefully was to be able to mark the beam positions and hatch openings, as we had expected to find much of the deck structure collapsed into the hull. In fact we found nothing and this puzzled us greatly until we discovered from Mersea man Bill Read that the majority of the deck had been cut out to accommodate the deckhouse when she was turned into a houseboat.

Shaun laid the framing out according to his hieroglyphics, and a pattern began to emerge. We had only one frame that went to the sheer-line in the first 25ft of the boat, or at least only one which we could place. Once that frame was positioned and some longitudinal battens were in place other frames started to fall into place. The top of the stem had been recovered complete with gammon iron and stemhead roller, but unfortunately we could not determine an exact height for the stem from the pieces we had. Shaun measured the stem of the *Vanduara*, which lays in a garden in Brightlingsea. From bobstay to covering board measured 5ft and from there to the top was another 3ft The top of the *Pioneer's* stem was only 4in different to *Vanduara's* so we reasoned that the distance from covering board to bobstay would be similar, a fact born out by the sheer batten when we sprang it round.

As if by magic, piece by piece the frames fell into place. After our success round the bow, we tackled the counter stern. We were very fortunate with the stern, we had just enough left to give us a shape. The counter had collapsed into the mud, and we had a great deal of trouble extracting the remnants. We had both quarter timbers, an arch board, some bits of horn timber and a short beam that was notched out to fit over the sternpost. We laid this all out on the ground and worked out a length for the beam in front of the sternpost. When a pattern of this beam was nailed onto the sternpost and the quarter timbers and archboard were erected we had a pretty good idea of the counter stern. Again after longitudinal battens were nailed up, the pieces of framing that we had saved fell into place. After a little fine tuning at the bow *Pioneer* was ready to have her lines taken properly.

At this time in the spring of 1999 we were also seeking trustees for the nascent charity, the *Pioneer Sailing Trust*. Apart from the immediate aim of saving the last deep water sailing dredger, the only surviving example of a well smack, and the only class one smack left that had been Colchester registered, the longer aims of the charity were being formed. When we first conceived the idea of digging *Pioneer* out of the mud we were look-ing no further than retrieving the bits with a view to rebuilding her at some time in the future. As we became more involved, and began to think more deeply about rebuilding the boat we realised that the boat would have to work when it was finished. The obvious use for her would be sail training, and it was to this end that we worked.

Our original group of three comprised, my boatbuilder colleague Shaun White, Rupert Marks, owner of the smack *Hyacinth* and me, Brian Kennell. Shaun and I could not be trustees, as boatbuilders we would be in charge of the work and earning money from the trust. The deed of trust would have to stipulate that no trustee took anything other than expens-es from the trust. Rupert would be a trustee, but three other trustees were required. One or two names sprang to mind and after an initial approach Charles Harker, owner of the bawley *Marigold* and lifelong enthusiast of traditional sail agreed to be one and Mary Falk, solicitor, single handed transatlantic sailor and former committee member of the International Sail Training Association agreed to be another.

A number of points needed to be sorted out about the reconstruction. Obviously having gone to all the trouble of digging her out of the mud we wished to rebuild her as faithfully to the original as possible. It's easy to say that a restoration will be "as authentic as possible" but right from the start compromises have to be made both in design and materials. *Pioneer's* wet well is an integral part of the boat, one of the reasons she is interest-ing. To earn her keep *Pioneer* has to take people sailing, but with 15ft of the middle taken up with the well, internal space would be severely restricted. The keel, deadwoods, stem and stern were originally oak and elm, and we planned to use oak and elm again if possible. Another factor to take into account is that when *Pioneer* was built it would have taken a matter of months. The rebuild would take several years. The oak that we obtain is fresh sawn and very prone to shrinkage and splitting in the ensu-ing years. Iroko is readily available and shrinks minimally as it seasons, but is not as environmentally friendly. We thought we may have to use it to obtain the sizes we would require, especially the keel. Other concessions that seemed likely to be made were the iron fastenings and fittings, again almost unobtainable and unfeasibly expensive.

Late in March, Rupert and his friend John Harding arranged to survey the complete boat for the definitive lines plan. Shaun and I were there to help and measure scantling sizes. John's sophisticated surveying equipment bounces a beam off a reflector held against the hull and back to the instrument. The distance is very accurately measured. Hundreds of these measurements had to be taken from a number of positions along the length of the boat. This information was then processed by John and passed on to David Cannell to be converted into a lines plan. Obviously this could have been done by old fashioned measurement, but it would have been a time consuming business. After the measurements were taken we covered her up to slow down the drying process and left her again.

Spring slowly turned into summer, we had a visit from Deanna Groom of St Andrews University, who have been given the job of preparing the Historic Ships Register. The Army thought they might be able to move *Pioneer* to Totham as an exercise, but then Kosovo got in the way. Sawmills were phoned at great length and patterns of frames were made. In April a tour of timberyards was made that took two days. We were primarily looking for oak bends for the grown oak frames of the boat, although other parts were also being sought: stem, sternpost, keel etc. The oak bends are difficult to find, they are the parts of the tree that are normally considered expendable and burnt on site. The curved frames of the boat are made up of bits of wood whose grain follows the shape – large branches and the crown of the tree normally supply them. John Barchard's old yard, now renamed Britannic Timber, was the first stop, but unfortunately they were too expensive to deal with. Adcocks at Corby Glen seemed more hopeful, I had dealt with them some years before and had found them very efficient.

That afternoon we visited the fishing museum in Grimsby. Its a difficult subject to cover and the museum trod a fine line between pleasing the casual visitor and acting as a national centre for the study of the history of fishing. We marvelled at the huge amount that had been spent on the buildings compared to the state of their vessels. The next day we visited two yards in Norfolk, Timb-a-Haul and Bob Wildin's. Both had useful looking material and seemed very helpful. It is a strange fact that most sawmills are tucked away down the most impossible country tracks, hidden from view and unadvertised, as if they are all members of some ancient order sworn to operate in secrecy.

Forming the charitable trust was proving to be a lengthier process than Rupert had thought. One of the sticking points was that because the boat was abandoned it was complicated to prove that we had clear title. If only we had a signed piece of paper from someone saying they had sold it to us. We had been told by several Mersea people that one of the local fishermen, Ronnie Garriock, had been given the wreck sometime in the '50s. Ronnie had been living in Spain for some years and it had seemed unlikely that he still had any claim to *Pioneer*, but we were in need of a seller and if he would sell us the wreck for a nominal sum it would serve the purpose. After much detective work Ronnie was run to ground in Suf-

folk, and agreed to sell the wreck along with a proper bill of sale, and a photograph of the boat signed by the previous owner.

About this time we had a bit of luck. Arthur Holt, a boatbuilder in Heybridge Basin was packing up and selling his equipment. We bought his work benches, cramps, trestles, blocks, quantities of wood and fastenings and a few power tools. This equipment formed the basis of our workshop at Great Totham.

On 7th July we went to Adcocks at Corby Glen. We took a trailer with us in expectation. My last dealings with Adcocks were some fifteen years previous but had been very successful. Richard Titchener and I had taken a lorry up to Corby Glen in the morning, Adcocks pulled out all the stops and by midday we had a lorry full of oak bends for the *Sallie*. We were not disappointed, Shaun and I found plenty of potential turns and once again Adcocks very efficiently cut them for us as we waited. The trailer was good for about two ton, by the end of the morning we had ten tons. As we left, we spotted Bob Wildin's lorry unloading oak in Adcock's field on the edge of the village. This meant that Bob Wildin was taking oak to Lincolnshire for us to export back down to Essex.

Towards the end of August Rupert collected a load of oak bends from Bob Wildin in Norfolk, the fruits of our efforts in the spring. We now had quite a large stack of wood for framing and it was decided to call a halt until we actually started work, although we were still on the look-out for tight turns for the floors. Another piece of good news that I got at about this time was that John Barchard had formed a new company called J.B. Timber, selling boatbuilding timber. We had been worried about finding a reliable supplier, especially for the planking, and it was reassuring to know John was back in business.

On the 23rd August we took down the battening and covers on the *Pioneer* in preparation for moving her up to Totham the next day. We had a young man called Brandon Oram helping us. He had contacted us earlier in the year about work, and we had agreed to give him a trial boat-building. He was full of enthusiasm and had come to give a hand to move her. At 8.00am on Tuesday 24th we gathered at Highams Farm in Gold-hanger, Rupert, Shaun and I were there as well as Brandon and Trustee Charles Harker. The same team that had moved her from Mersea were to move her up to Rupert's barn in Great Totham: Cadman Crane hire and Anglia Heavy Haulage.

By 11.30 she was loaded and waiting for the police escort. I went ahead to show the crane the way up to the barn at Totham, and to check that my colleague from work, Arthur Keeble, was set up with his lifting gear. Taking *Pioneer* off the lorry at Totham was going to be made diffi-cult by the dutch barn she was to go under. This meant the crane could not lift her conventionally with two strops. The plan was to block up under the keel immediately behind the lorry. The crane would lift the other end of the keel, which just projected beyond the barn. Arthur had set up his chain hoists and strops in the middle of the barn to hold her upright. Once she was lifted clear of the lorry it would drive out, and due to the height of the trailer she would then have to be lowered closer to the ground.

Of course, we did not even know at that point that we could get the lorry from the main road up two fields into the barn. The police escort was late and it was lunchtime before she arrived at the lay-by opposite the fields she had to negotiate to get to the barn. Presently the tractor arrived that would assist the lorry up the fields. The driver of the lorry decided to try and get as far as he could without the tractor, which was not very far. There was a nasty moment when the tractor was shackled to the lorry and its wheels started to spin, but soon the whole train was under way and in no time *Pioneer* was in the barn.

All went well initially, the pile of sleepers were built under the keel at the bow and the crane took the weight under the heel. The laborious job of lowering her down from 5ft off the floor to about 2ft 6in began. This was achieved by lowering her a bit at the bow with a jack, then lowering away on the crane at the stern. Meanwhile Arthur lowered away on the chainhoists that kept her upright. These hoists were not capable of bearing more than 2-3 tons, so we had to be careful to lower away before they became overloaded. Whilst this process was going on the keel began to bend quite alarmingly. After a particularly sickening lurch accompanied by cracking and a worried cry from Arthur that she was breaking up, we had to scurry about and block up under the centre of the keel to stop her falling in two. From this point on we had to employ two jacks to lower her with. An onlooker said the keel deflected over a foot before we managed to block the keel. Finally she was securely blocked and shored, and a well earned glass of champagne was downed.

The next landmark was a month later when David Cannell and his assistant James Pratt came to Totham to show us the draft lines plan. The lines were remarkably fair considering the way they had been obtained, and we all speculated about the skill of the boatbuilders who had so competently lengthened her. To lengthen a boat by 11ft is more difficult than it first appears. Firstly the point where the boat is largest has to be identified, then the boat is cut in two at this point. In *Pioneer's* case the wet well formed the new centre of the boat. We knew that *Pioneer's* keel had probably been replaced at this time, two pieces of elm, scarphed together just forward of the mast-step. We were perplexed as to how they had managed to make the planking fair-in from the old ends of the boat to the new middle, without ending up with a flat spot somewhere.

Two weeks later in early October I showed Deanna Groom and her boss Dr Robert Prescott of St Andrews University over the *Pioneer*, and whilst examining her I realized how they had faired the hull so successfully. We think that *Pioneer* was almost completely re-planked when she was lengthened. The aft wet well bulkhead, installed at this time, is the same as the framing at this point. The forward bulkhead is larger and the frames forward of it have been packed out. When she was replanked, the planking faired out round the larger forward bulkhead and packed out frames, increasing her sections around the mainmast and towards the bow. This cleverly preserved her run aft and increased her "body" forward, thus ensuring the balance of the hull was not lost.

The reason we thought that the planking had been replaced was the lack of trenails, despite there being plenty of trenails in the framing. Trenails, commonly pronounced "trunnels", are wooden nails. Between 1864 when *Pioneer* was built and 1889 when she was lengthened, trenails must have been superseded by iron spikes. I feel sure that, like many improvements, iron spikes were not necessarily better but cheaper. Our experience of trenails is that they are very long lived fastenings, iron spikes are attacked by the gallic and tannic acids in oak. More recently galvanised steel has replaced iron for fastenings, unfortunately steel is even more prone to attack by the acids in oak.

Obviously a great deal of oak would be going into the rebuild. Since the iron originally used to fasten her up was now unobtainable, and steel fastenings would start to need replacing after 30 years, bronze seemed the only other option. Bronze is expensive, but there are advantages. Bronze is unaffected by the acids in oak, is very resistant to corrosion in the marine environment, and should be good for 70-80 years or more before it

Fitting the new Keel

needs replacement. Bronze does not affect the wood around it either, unlike steel which will decay the wood as it itself decays. It also has an advantage over steel, which needs to be sent away for galvanizing after fitting or thread cutting. This can create delays and over the course of the whole job would be quite expensive. Nickel aluminium bronze would be used for the keel bolts and other bolts throughout the boat, as it is stronger than steel. The spikes would be phospher bronze, supplied by the Glasgow Steel Nail Co.

By now it was late October, Brandon and another young man called

Alex Risk had already been working for a month setting up the workshop and attaching the heavy covers that were turning the dutch barn into a weatherproof shed. Shaun and I had nearly completed other outstanding work and were ready to start. We had been promised wood for the keel any day, and so we started stripping the old internal lining from the hull to reveal the concrete. Concrete was very common in smacks when they were built, the purpose was to fill between the framing and form a smooth inner surface for the lining to fit against. All water in the bilge of the boat then runs back to a sump between two frames. We started using electric breakers to remove the concrete from between the frames, revealing odd bits of scrap-iron, including a cannon ball.

On 28th October the keel arrived, along with wood for the wet well bulkheads. The keel is opepe and the bulkheads are elm, as before. The keel was also originally elm and although elm of that size was no longer available we had hoped to use oak. Paradoxically we discovered that the dimensions of the keel were too small to use oak. The keel is 15in deep by 7in wide and it would have been too risky to try and "box the heart" as timber suppliers say. This means that the heart of the tree is in the centre of the keel and at 7in wide *Pioneer's* keel was too narrow to be able to reliably do this. The next job was to block the boat up so that the keel was hanging unsupported and set Brandon off with a reciprocating saw to cut through the old keel bolts. This was accomplished without too much trouble (although Brandon might disagree) despite most of the bolts being in very good condition.

Shaun marking out a floor timber

The new keel would be just like the 1889 replacement, scarphed about 15ft back from the stem. We set the new keel parts up next to the old keel, which Rupert and Brandon had dragged out from under the old boat with the tractor. The new wood had to be planed and one of the Trust's firsts purchases was a portable electric planer 12in wide. This machine earned its keep on the keel alone, saving days of work. Cutting and temporarily bolting the two halves followed. The rebate for the planking to join the keel had to be cut next. Shaun and I decided to use the old rebate for a pattern, as it was in good order and at that stage we did not have any reliable drawings. It took three weeks for us to make the keel, which we slid under the boat on the 30th November. We marked the laying of the keel – the start of the restoration – with Champagne.

It was the work of afew days to set the boat down on its new keel, straightening it out as we did so. Along with the keel, elm for the wet well bulkheads had been delivered. We thought it would be a good idea to rough the three bulkheads out, as the elm was freshly sawn and would start to dry more quickly if it were cut to size. The hope was that when we came to fit the bulkheads the wood would have stabilized. Also we would know whether we had enough elm for the three bulkheads. At this stage we were still planning to fit the bulkheads as if the wet well was to be properly fitted. This meant that the sections making up the bulkheads would have the double tongues in the seams, and stopwaters between bulkheads and keel, and stopwaters in the plank seams in way of the bulkheads.

Before Christmas we made and cut out the new stem. It was 12ft tall and required an extension on the jib of the tractor to lift into place. Once the stem was set up the full size of *Pioneer* became apparent, even those of us who knew what to expect were impressed. Next came the sternpost, and after that we removed all of the old boat forward of the wet well. This left the front of the boat looking very naked apart from the stem. Logically the next move would be to cut the old stern off as well, and then set up the deadwoods forward and aft. Unfortunately this would mean that very little of the old boat would be left for visitors to see, so we decided to concentrate on the bow of the boat, framing from the wet well to the stem first.

James Pratt, assistant to naval architect David Cannell, produced the definitive lines plan of *Pioneer*. The architects had digitally compared a photograph of *Pioneer* at the turn of the century with later photos and the preliminary lines plan, and had been able to adjust the sheer to its former sweep. The keel had also been straightened with the aid of the computer, and it was the hope that lofting the shape of the frames could be simplified by using full size patterns, generated by computer. This

looked to be an excellent system, saving many hours of work drawing the shape of each frame on the loft floor. We started to frame at the forward end of the wet well, moving towards the bow. It had been difficult to work out how the original frames had been set out, as extra frames had been added over the years until *Pioneer* had virtually no gaps between them. Shaun and I decided on a simple 8 inch gap, with the frames built of two 4 ½ inch oak parts side by side. This will mean that she is at least as heavily framed as she was originally.

At the end of January we paid a visit to the Excelsior Trust in Lowestoft. John Wylson gave us a guided tour of *Excelsior*, a Lowestoft sailing trawler that the trust restored to sailing condition about ten years ago, and the *City of Edinboro'*. *City of Edinboro'* is a large Hull trawler built in the 1870s. In recent years she has had a chequered career and it is fortunate she has fallen into the hands of the *Excelsior* trust. We were impressed by the standard of the restoration on *Excelsior*, and the level of commitment to authenticity by John Wylson.

Wood for framing was becoming a problem again, and there had been word of a nice parcel of larch suitable for planking. Adcock's at Corby Glen in Lincolnshire thought they might have some more oak suitable for bends. The larch belonged to John Barchard and was about another half hours drive away at John Hall's yard at Bleasby in Nottinghamshire, so it was decided that Shaun and I would spend a day timber hunting. Adcock's were in the process of setting up at a new location outside the village and they were very disorganised. It took until mid-afternoon to saw afew

New and Old. Looking towards the bow, showing original well

bends, and it was touch and go whether we went on to Bleasby. Because of our lack of success so far we decided to make the effort. The first thing that greets the visitor to John Hall's sawmill is a steam crane overgrown with brambles. Other old plant lies apparently abandoned, but knowing John's resourcefulness, it probably isn't. In amongst this and the mud was some of the nicest larch we had seen for years. At this point I should say that John Hall's yard is not unusual for a sawmill, most of them run on a wing and a prayer, and only exist due to the dedication of their owners. The larch had all come from the same source, the edge of a castle moat in south Wales. Planted late in the nineteenth century on the slope, most of the logs had some sweep in them as they had fought to grow upright.

The following week Rupert, Shaun and I returned to John Hall's to select some larch and see it sawn. The bandsaw is a large horizontal machine and John claims it is the oldest saw working in the country, built in the north of England in 1913. We selected 14 trees which we hoped would be ample for the planking. All the trees were of high quality, with close annular rings and few knots. The majority of the planks are 2in thick, with some at 3in for the wale and the turn of the bilge. Some of the logs were straight the rest had up to 9in of bend in them. We had calculated the maximum amount of bend we might need and we had trees with anything from the maximum to straight, anything from 25ft long to 40ft long.

Towards the end of March, Rupert, Charles, Shaun, my wife Sally and I visited the Public Records Office at Kew. We were searching for references to *Pioneer*, especially around 1948 when she was withdrawn from the register. Kew is a confusing place due to the sheer quantity of material they have, and you have to know exactly what you are looking for, and it is quite difficult to find out what Kew actually has. We found a good deal of information in the 1948 files, the year that she was deregistered. This included details of the steam winch of 1925 and engine installed in 1929, an Atlantic of 35 hp. We also discovered something called the "Annual Fishing Boat Returns". These documents are a yearly record of what every registered fishing boat in every port in Britain was doing. They were started in 1895 and ran at least until the second world war. Boats are listed chronologically by fishing number. We discovered that *Pioneer* had been dredging, employing six men, throughout the 1890s. By the 1930s she was marked down as unemployed despite the engine installed in 1929. We found out a great deal, but in the process realized how much more information there was to be had if we could find the time to retrieve it. For instance there has to be more information about past owners and masters hiding in the files.

Back in Totham framing continued apace. By April the framing forward of the wet well was finished. It was decided to leave the wet well until last, concentrating on the aft end of the boat next. Remnants of the old framing and the deadwood were cut off and the new deadwood was drilled and set up. The longest keelbolt in the aft deadwood is over 5ft long. By this stage wood for framing was in short supply again and after another abortive trip to Norfolk, more oak was obtained from John Barchard, our saviour for oak bends.

The Trustees had decided it would be a good idea to hold an open day. June 17th was chosen, a Saturday. It was a great success with an estimated 200 or more people turning up to view progress, have a cup of tea and chat. Generally people were impressed with the scale of the job and were supportive with their donations and offers of help.

By the end of June framing was complete to the top of the sternpost and it was time to think about the counter stern. I was away during July, so Shaun set up the horn timbers and quarter timbers and had started the rudder trunk by the time I returned. The skill involved in setting up these components is not to be underestimated. This part of the boat had almost totally disappeared in the mud, and the naval architects had not attempted to draw the counter stern. The rudder trunk is round in section, made of douglas fir and held together with softwood tongues. It was decided to glue the trunk together, as it was vital that it does not leak.

I continued with the wet well bulkheads, fitting the large slabs of elm together and routing them out for the double softwood tongues that would have originally made them watertight. Finally the last part of the old boat had to be removed. Again the poor tractor was called to lift far more than it was designed to, but with three people standing on the back it was persuaded to remove the old bulkheads. By mid September the three new bulkheads were installed, and the last frames were going in. The wet well deck originally projected to the outside of the hull, with the planking rebating round it. We have recreated this feature in the new wet well with huge oak boards 5in thick by 12in wide running round either side of the boat. On top of these pieces there are 5in square clamps bolted to them and to the framing. This makes *Pioneer* extremely strong amidships on the waterline. This strength compensates for the keelson not running through the wet well area. The final short frames were added to the wet well tops, and the framing was finished.

Planking is the next job. It was the end of November and we were still on target time-wise. To maintain our schedule we would need to complete the planking in eight months. First Shaun and I had to decide the sheer-line. A rough line was obtained from the plans, which we faired in

80

with long battens. Unless a boat is built in the middle of a field it is an act of faith striking the sheer in, as you need to stand well back to check for flat spots and humps. We would just have to wait until the boat came out of the shed.

Most people assume that planking starts at the bottom and works its way up to the top, which is true of some types of construction, but not *Pioneer's*. The top plank, or sheerstrake, is the first, followed by the two wale planks. The wale, at 3in thick is an inch thicker than most of the rest of the planks. Nearly every plank needs to be steamed, and we were experimenting with a new method introduced to us by David Patient – "boil-in-the-bag". The first real test of the new method was the top wale plank, which had to be twisted through 90 degrees from the topsides to the underside of the counter stern. This went very well and has saved us many hours and a lot of effort. After we had fitted the top four planks it was time to move down to the bottom plank, the garboard.

It was also Christmas and time for our works party. Rupert treated the team to a meal at The Butley Oysterage at Orford. The whole outing was a great success and nine hours later Rupert returned me to Maldon a little the worse for wear.

In the New Year James Green joined the team.

The beginning of 2001 saw planking started. Soon we fell into a rhythm, Shaun and James mainly working on the port side, Brandon and I the starboard side. As winter turned to spring the planking slowly marched up the stem and sternpost. The steamer, after initial troubles was behaving well. In its final form it was a beer barrel, heated by 6 immersion heaters and 2 gas burners. The "boil in the bag" method of steaming has proved to be very successful, saving time and effort.

The well stringer that goes right through to the outside of the planking

Less successful was the computer generated framing. This had not been able to cope with the run aft and the "tuck" where the planking reaches the top of the sternpost and joins the rudder trunk, resulting in much work for the boatbuilders. Next came fitting the planks round the wet well top, and finally the shutter (last) plank, just above the turn of the bilge. This was accomplished by the middle of August.

During the spring 2001 we were visited by Bob Stoker, now in his nineties, along with his friend "Cromer Crab" of similar vintage and David Stoker, Bob's son. Bob clearly remembered *Pioneer* and regaled us with tales of pre-war stowboating on *Priscilla*, his smack. We all had a jolly couple of hours chatting and it was with great sadness we learnt of his death afew weeks later.

Fairing up the hull followed fitting the final plank. This involves much hand work to obtain a pleasing finish to the hull, and is probably one of the most physically demanding jobs on the boat. I went on holiday. Lastly, the first plank fitted, the oak sheerstrake, had its temporary fastenings removed and was refitted and refastened. This was necessary due to the amount it had shrunk over the last eight months.

To go back a little, July 7th had been our second open day, with many more visitors than the first. Jamie Dodds, a local artist who is rapidly making a name for himself for the quality of his paintings and linocuts, donated a linocut of *Pioneer* for raffle. This along with the many generous donations raised over £1,000. More importantly it was a chance to publicise the project, and allow people to view the work. And view it they did, with around 500 people coming to see us and have a chat.

By the end of September the beamshelf was in and bolted. Shaun and I breathed a sigh of relief at that. Scarphed amidships either side, the four huge chunks of larch that comprised this member had taken 5 hours apiece to steam into position and many more hours to fit and bolt. For those who do not know, the beamshelf is literally what it says, a shelf for the deck beams to sit on. Cutting out the massive oak beams, 6in x 4in in section, followed.

More of *Pioneer's* history surfaced in the autumn when I was contacted by Joe French of Brightlingsea. He and his brother remembered going aboard *Pioneer* when they were children. Arthur French, his father, skippered *Pioneer* once for Tom Poole, who owned her in the 1920's. He clearly remembered sitting in front of the capstan boiler drying his feet. He also recollects Tom chasing his father up the road and pleading with him to take *Pioneer* for a voyage and his father reluctantly agreeing. Joe also explained why *Pioneer* and her three sisters, which were all owned by Tom, finished fishing at the same time. Tom had a store next to the electricity generating station and hot exhaust gases set Tom's store alight along with all his smacks sails and running rigging. This was in about 1929 and after this only the *Fiona* was left to carry on into the early thirties.

About this time in early October Rupert, Shaun and I had a day out on the south coast. Apart from afew interesting houseboats at Shoreham the most interesting find was the Maritime museum at Newhaven. Incongruously positioned at an out of town shopping centre, it was everything a museum should be in my opinion. The walls were crammed with paintings and photographs, display cabinets bulged with interesting artefacts, and, most interesting for us were the albums. There were more than fifty of them, full of post cards and photos that had been donated. There was no time to look at them all, but we did find a lovely photo of *Victor* CK 31 lying alongside in Newhaven harbour. *Victor* being a similar size to *Pioneer* before she was lengthened, she is noted along with *Pioneer* as being in Newhaven at the time of the 1881 census.

November and December came and went. Beams, lodging knees, covering boards and stanchions were fitted and fixed. In the New Year we reorganised ourselves with Jim Green and Brandon putting the lining in whilst Shaun and I tackled the counter stern and rudder respectively. Originally *Pioneer* was fully lined inside with 2in thick pine. We planned to line the upper part of the interior, leaving lower open for ventilation purposes. We used 2in larch for this with close seams, ie no caulking seam.

Metalwork needed making and it was decided to ask a semi-retired blacksmith from Brightlingsea to help out getting us started. And so Keith Ruffle came to show our resident metalworker how to forge steel. Unfortunately iron of any quality proved too difficult to source. Steel is much harder and consequently more difficult to work. Alex developed muscles in places he did not know he was meant to have muscles. It has been all-worthwhile and some of *Pioneer's* fittings are bordering on art-work.

By spring our thoughts were definitely turning to the deck planking. This material had been debated at great length for what seemed like years. It had finally been decided to award the contract to supply the decking, machined to size, to Capricorn Timber of Uttoxeter, who in turn were sourcing Columbian pine from North America. We placed the order and sat back and waited . . .

Other elements of the job were slowly wound up. Shaun finished the counter stern, I finished the rudder and carved the name board, Brandon planked the well top and James got on with the watertight bulkheads. Rail boarding was fitted and stemhead fittings were planned. The boat was weighed to help the naval architect with his calculations. This was done with load cells for weighing Jumbo jets. We all bet that she would be about 30 tons, so it was with surprise we found her to be only 20 tons. This slightly upset us as we definitely felt that we had carried more than 20 tons of wood up the steps aboard *Pioneer*. We began to fidget about the decking . . .

Early in May Rupert, Shaun and I set off to look at the deck timber at Capricorn Timber in Derbyshire. We had never seen such nice wood with growth rings so close. What was disappointing was the size of the rough sawn timber, which was very near the finished size that we needed. However, Roger the boss assured us that all would be well. We returned to Essex and eagerly awaited its arrival . . .

By the middle of June we were desperate, unless we got the decking soon it would jeopardise our provisional launch date of September 21st. The decking arrived and our worst fears were confirmed, the machining had not been successful and a good deal of our beautiful decking was unusable. We needed the decking to be at least 2in thick to match the covering board. About half of the wood was too thin.

Drastic action was necessary, nothing could be done quickly as more wood needed to be imported from North America. Rupert cancelled the launch date, whilst Shaun, James and Alex caulked and stopped *Pioneer* up. Then Shaun and I cut the waterline in and put several coats of paint

Midships, looking forward to the well bulkheads

on the hull to protect her as best we could from shrinkage and we bade her farewell for the winter.

To keep our spirits up we had two trips out in December. The first visit was to Lowestoft Maritime Museum, a small volunteer run place next to the beach. It is just the sort of museum I like, full of models and artefacts with local relevance. Someone had kindly come and opened the hall up specially, they even demonstrated the cased clockwork model of a Lowestoft smack which heaves and pitches on a canvas sea in a most realistic fashion. That afternoon we met Jim Barnard, a retired Lowestoft trawlerman now in his nineties. His recollections of working between the wars on sailing trawlers and steam trawlers were both interesting and informative.

Our Christmas outing saw Rupert, Shaun, Jim and I set off for a tour of the Medway. Although interesting, places we wished to see were closed and people we visited were out. It was all in danger of collapse when someone hit on the idea of going to Wheelers Oyster Bar in Whitstable for a meal. Another place that I can highly recommend. We perched on stools in the window and goggled at the selection of seafood on display. The only solution to our dilemma was to ask for "a platter with a bit of everything on it between the four of us". Several hours later with all of us bulging over our belts and three of our number awash with wine from the off licence opposite we headed home.

With the first signs of spring came the first signs of returning shipwrights. Familiar faces appeared in the early morning gloom. As well as myself Shaun White, Jim Green and our "lad" Ben Cox started to pick up the threads.

The re-machined and replaced wood had arrived in December ready for our

New deck: last glimpse of the topside of the deck beams lodging knees.

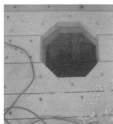

left: The bow. right: Details of new deck being laid, fitting gammon iron to stem head

start in early February. Laying a deck progresses much more quickly than planking, all the wood is straight and parallel with a caulking seam machined onto it. The tops of the beams need to be faired so the decking lays nicely on them, but there is no steaming or bending involved. The most difficult parts are in the initial setting out when the plank widths are decided and cutting the planks in at the stern and round the deck fittings.

There were other fittings that needed to be fitted and bolted on, mizzen chainplates and stemhead snatch with the roller, but the largest job other than decking was the keel band. Back during the previous summer Alex had made a steel mould for manufacturing the straight sections of keel band in lead. This mould was about six feet long and would use up all the scrap lead that had been donated to the trust. The appeal for scrap lead had been very successful and most of the keel band, all 3 tons, was made from it.

Ben and Rupert perfected a system for melting and pouring the half ton of lead required for each section of band. Lead has to be cast all in one go, otherwise you end up with something that looks like a wafer biscuit and delaminates like one too. After a couple of false starts they got the hang of it and by the last one Ben could make a section on his own in two days. Ben then had the not inconsiderable job of fitting the keel to the boat. This involved manoeuvring each section under the boat and jacking it into place. Ben's father Tom built a framework to go on a pallet truck to assist in this operation. Each section is held on with big bronze coach-screws. Perhaps the strangest part of this job was watching Ben planing the tops of the keel band with the big power planer, for lead can be worked in a similar fashion to wood. Moulds had been made for the ends of the keel, and these had been caste in bronze as we felt this would wear better.

By late March caulking started. Willing volunteers rolled yards of oakum and the shed rang to the merry tap of mallet on iron. The seams needed to be filled with pitch on top of the oakum and more ingenuity came into play. One of the main problems with pitching is when the pitch becomes too hot and boils in the pitchpot, this can result in aeration and can also alter the properties of the pitch causing it to become brittle. We discovered that a deep fat fryer was excellent for the job, keeping the pitch simmering perfectly.

Rupert had set a launch date of the 17th. May and we set to with the final jobs. Debbie Cannom was in charge of painting, she and a team of several helpers producing a nice glossy finish. Black topsides and rail boarding, red bottom, cream rail capping with a darker buff inside the rail and grey decks all set off with a bright yellow cove line. There was some debate whether to paint or oil the deck, but in the end we decided that paint offered better protection against the elements.

Something else that had been nagging away for some time was how would we get her to the water? We planned to launch her on Brightlingsea hard which was not the closest, but was the best for spectators and would return her to her home for much of her working life. Anglia Heavy Haulage had put her in the shed and had thought they would be able to get her out again. Height turned out to be a problem though as we worked out that she could only be 12in off the ground at times to clear power cables, most notably the overhead lines at Eastgates railway crossing in Colchester. This gain in height was due to the new stem which stood nearly 13ft above the keel. Only a month before the launching date we were looking for a specialist haulier to move her. Several false starts were made, but in the end we contacted Abbey Transport of Norwich.

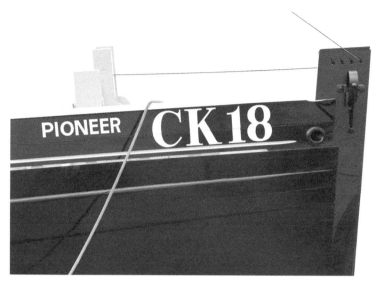

The other great plan was to put her on a specially constructed trailer on Brightlingsea hard and launch her with a splash at tide time, using a traction engine to haul her down. This plan died due to its enormous cost and risk of failure and the awful possibility that we might drop *Pioneer*.

Although Abbey transport could carry her only 12in from the ground, she had to be raised 36in from the ground to drive the trailer, which was 9ft wide, underneath her. We could not use a crane as she was in a barn. A week before launch day we set-to with four large hydraulic jacks and jacked her to 48in off the concrete. We then slid long steel beams under her and blocked them up at their ends to enable the trailer to drive right under her.

The plan was that we would load *Pioneer* on the Wednesday. She would then be taken to Colchester on Wednesday evening and parked outside the Castle Park Gates until Friday evening when she would make the journey to Brightlingsea. Saturday morning she would be craned onto the hard ready to float about an hour before high water. The idea of taking her to Colchester was to raise local awareness of the project.

Wednesday morning dawned grey, we hoped it would not rain as the lorry had to drive over two fields to get to the main road. The Trust had been kindly loaned some aluminium roadway to lay down the field if the ground was too soft to drive on. This came complete with a 24 hour guard as it was worth a small fortune. Abbey Transport arrived at about ten with their huge trailer. This trailer could be extended to accommodate a long keel boat like *Pioneer* and incorporated a hydraulic jacking system to raise or lower the boat. It was also possible to steer the five back axles for getting into tight spots. Soon the four strong Abbey team, assisted by eight Pioneer Trust men were beavering away to lower *Pioneer* onto the trailer. Just as we were all beginning to breath a sigh of relief misfortune struck in the shape of an intense hail storm. Onlookers scuttled for cover and we cursed our bad luck, as this meant a good deal of hard work laying the portable road across the field. This would have to be done in relays as the lorry crawled along, picking up the sheets behind the lorry and putting them down ahead for it to drive onto.

Slowly the *Pioneer* inched out of her home for the last three years until she stood resplendent in the watery sunshine on the first section of roadway. A dramatic turn of events now took place.

Mindful that we would be there late into the evening moving the roadway down the field, the Abbey driver took a unilateral decision and drove forward off the roadway and into the field. Gunning the engine of the huge tractor unit he went about a length and a half into the barley crop before he lost traction and stopped. The rain started to fall again.

At this point there was a definite schism and opinion fell into two camps, the breezy optimism of the Abbey Transporters and the deep gloom of the rest of us at the potentially enormous task ahead. Rupert

Emerging from the shed

alone had reached a high level of anxiety only to be guessed at by the rest of us. One of the most bizarre moments of the day for me occurred at this point. I looked up the rain sodden field and spotted a small figure perched in the middle at the top of a very tall stepladder, looking totally incongruous. This turned out to be Mervyn Maggs, the photographer who has been recording progress for the last few years.

A tractor was requested and the whole caravan slithered forwards another length. A second tractor was added and a little more ground was covered. Rupert engaged in frantic phone calls, and like the cavalry arriving, tractors appeared from several different directions. The four most powerful were harnessed to the lorry with the fifth one out in front tooting his horn. The testosterone was almost tangible. Clutches were engaged and the whole lot shot off down the fields with the rest of us trailing behind running for all our worth.

When we arrived at the main road the tractor drivers were animatedly totting up how many horsepower it had taken to move *Pioneer*. By eight o'clock the police escort had arrived and we were on the move again. At 15ft wide *Pioneer* filled the whole road but progress was smooth and we hit the outskirts of Colchester at dusk. Once in the town the only hitch was negotiating the turn from Head Street into the High Street, with the counter stern sweeping within inches of the first floor windows. The *Pioneer* was reversed into the crescent outside the Park Gates literally in a trice and by nine o'clock the first stage of the journey was over.

Preparations for the launch went ahead, fenders and mooring warps had to be organised. We had some huge warps that had been kindly donated by Chris Stopford, skipper of a large motor yacht in the Mediterranean. Chris thought they had a breaking strain of 70 tons, more than adequate! Her position on the hard had to be worked out so that she would float about an hour and a half before high water. Rupert did some calculations which he hoped would be accurate.

Meanwhile, fund raising and publicity in Colchester were going well. It was interesting to see how people reacted to seeing *Pioneer* in her unusual position. Passers by paused to stare, whole bus loads of people craned their necks, but equally there were those determined not to acknowledge that she was there at all. She was just an irritating obstruction to their progress through the park gates. Best reaction of all was the Traffic Warden who seriously considered putting a ticket on the lorry.

Friday evening Abbey Transport again swung into action and again seemingly without effort started the journey towards Brightlingsea. It was a grey evening and our convoy was late arriving, but as we breasted the hill by Brightlingsea church the first group of people came into view at the side of the road. By the time we arrived at the waterside the streets were alive with onlookers. All that remained was to park *Pioneer* up for the night and try and get some sleep to be ready for a 5.30am start.

Saturday morning dawned wet and cold. The lorry reversed down the hard and positioned itself close to the scrubbing posts. Two cranes from Cannon Crane Hire were to be used for the lift. Two cranes are more controlled and give a kinder lift on the boat, also it means that you do not need such big cranes. The lift went smoothly and *Pioneer* was set down with her legs in place to hold her upright. Legs were regularly used when the boats worked as a simple way of keeping a boat upright when scrubbing the bottom and painting. Mooring lines were secured, about 4 tons of ballast were added and surprisingly quickly the water arrived.

The poor weather failed to keep the crowds away, Colne Community School band struck up late in the morning and people jostled for a better view. I estimate that there were getting on for a thousand onlookers. Whilst I and the others charged with looking after the boat fretted about the next part of the plan which involved moving her onto the Yacht Club pontoon so that the crowd could get a close up look, Rupert and Charles shepherded the dignitaries down to the *Boy George*. *Boy George* is a bumkin, a small open oyster boat from West Mersea. She is owned by retired boatbuilder John Milgate. *Boy George* ferried the great and good aboard and we all hoped that Rupert's tidal calculations were correct.

Right on cue, *Pioneer* floated and we hauled her round to the jetty so she could be viewed by the crowd. Thick and fast the visitors came aboard, at one point I counted 60 people on deck. So popular was the chance to see aboard that we were late moving her back on the hard and we had quite a struggle to moor her athwart the ebb tide. By the time she had settled it was late afternoon and the reception in the Colne Yacht Club was nearly

Offloading onto Brightlingsea Town Hard

over. Fortunately some of the wine and oysters had been saved for us. The previous few days had been highly charged emotionally for me and I felt totally drained and exhausted. It was with relief that I fell into my bunk on the *Sallie* that night.

On the Sunday we moved *Pioneer* out onto the end pontoon in the harbour with the assistance of the Brightlingsea harbour master. During the summer we installed the ballast and concrete and she was painted below. We also visited Capricorn Timber in Uttoxeter and selected the douglas fir for the masts and spars. The wood was imported from Canada for the job so all the spars could be made from single pieces, with no gluing or scarphing. Largest is the mainmast at over 50ft long and 11in in diameter. She also had two outings to local events. Firstly she attended the Rowhedge Regatta, laying overnight on the mud opposite the village. Later, in September she laid in the Victory dock at West Mersea for a weekend Essex Seafood Festival and many Mersea visitors came to see her there.

By October it was getting time to think of laying *Pioneer* in a mud berth for the winter. Between the Colne Smack Dock and the commercial wharf there is a perfect berth for her. Rupert negotiated with the owners and obtained agreement that she could lay there for what we hope is the first of many winters.

Currently at the end of 2003 Shaun and I are making the masts and spars for *Pioneer* and it is hoped she will be sailing by next summer.

Pioneer in her winter mud berth

Shaun and Brian making the main mast

THE LAUNCH

By Charles Harker

The First Class Essex Smack *Pioneer* CK18 has just made the most extraordinary journey of her 140 year lifetime.

With her hull and deck completed it was important to get her into the water before the heat of the Summer opened up her seams. Arrangements were therefore made to transport her by road from Scripps Farm, Gt Totham to Brightlingsea which was her home port throughout her long working life.

The haulage contract was undertaken by Messrs Abbey Ltd of Norwich who handled the whole operation most professionally. The main problem was to find a trailer long and low enough to take the 70ft long and 14ft 9in high hull. Minimum clearance on the route was 15ft 4in.

Abbey Ltd arrived at Scripps Farm with a crew of 4 tough looking truckers and some awesome equipment. There was an 80ton Iveco tractor unit towing a new Commetto extendable 5 axle low loading trailer. This has a full power rear steerage unit and extends to 26m and can load 60 tons. The *Pioneer* at this stage weighs 23tons. In addition they brought a 150 ton F16 tractor unit and a support vehicle to head the convoy.

The *Pioneer* had already been jacked onto RSJs blocked up at each side clear of the hull. The trailer was reversed under the ship and hydraulically raised to take her weight. The RSJs were then removed and the *Pioneer* was secured onto the trailer which was then lowered. Ground clearance was minimal.

Whilst this 3 hour operation took place a thunderstorm broke. The sky darkened, rain and hail lashed the *Pioneer's* shed. Water ran in torrents down the Farm drive – and soaked the field of wheat over which the *Pioneer* had to travel before reaching a metalled road. We had anticipated the risk and Anglian Water kindly loaned some aluminium decking. We had about 40 sections each 5 metres long to lay in relay before the lorry as she crossed the 1000 metre field. Abbey, however chose to attempt the crossing with out the decking. The driver took a run at it, got 20 metres, and stuck! We put a single tractor on the lorries head with no success then another and another. The *Pioneer* was hard ashore on the Totham Banks. But then even bigger and more powerful tractors appeared. At last 4 great beasts were coupled up side by side. Engines roared and belched black smoke. The *Pioneer* lurched forward and as if reluctant to leave the home where she had been so carefully restored set off down the field. She gathered speed and with a crowd running behind the whole yoke swept out onto the Colchester Road.

Later the *Pioneer* set off for Colchester. A police escort headed the convoy,
blue lights flashing followed by the support vehicle. Then came the *Pioneer*,
her 15ft beam filling the narrow road. A
queue of traffic followed on behind.
The *Pioneer* was driven into Colchester
as darkness fell. The tight nip at the top
of Head Street took 20 minutes to clear.
The town came to a standstill. She then
rolled majestically passed the Town
Hall before parking up in the Crescent
in front of Colchester Castle.

The *Pioneer* spent the next two
days on view. Her presence in the centre
of Town reaffirmed her links with
Colchester, her port of registry, a town
associated with the oyster trade since
the Romans. The Deputy Mayor of
Colchester, Councillor John Bouckley
and his wife came aboard. Alex Midlen
of the Colne Estuary Partnership
brought a European deputation from
the Maritime Heritage Trust to view
the ship.

100

On Friday evening the *Pioneer* started on her final leg of the journey to Brightlingsea. As she climbed the hill past All Saints Church a crowd of people greeted her. And from there on all along the route to the Hard people waved and cheered. It was a grand "Welcome Home".

Early on Saturday morning the *Pioneer* was reversed down the Hard. Two cranes supplied by R. J. Cannon of Tiptree swung her off the trailer. Supported on her own legs the *Pioneer* rested on Brightlingsea Hard for the first time for at least 70 years.

Out in the Creek a fleet of smacks and bawleys had gathered to watch the launch. The *Sallie* and the *My Alice* from Maldon, the *Mary* from Kent lay alongside the *Ellen* and the *Saxonia*. Dressed overall they made a brave sight. The *Bona* got underway with a crowd aboard and the Cirdan Sailing Trust's *Xylonite* sailed proudly into the creek to anchor off the wharf. It all recalled a bygone age.

101

left: *Alan Goggin*. Right: *Mary Falk, Alan Goggin, Janet Russell, Jo Ruffel, Rupert Marks & Charles Harker*

At 11.30 hrs the launching party gathered on the Yacht Club jetty. John and Angus Milgate sailed them in the bumkin *Boy George* off to the *Pioneer* which by now was surrounded by water.

Crowds gathered on the foreshore. The Band of the Colne Community School played rousing nautical airs. As the *Pioneer* waited to float a 15ft pennant donated by James Lawrence Sailmakers flew gaily over her.

Charles Harker, Trustee of the *Pioneer Sailing Trust* addressed the company and thanked the people of Brightlingsea for their warm welcome. He acknowledged the Trust's debt to so many people who had made this day possible.

Councillor Janet Russell, Mayor of Brightlingsea said this was her first duty as Mayor and a proud day for the Town which once numbered her fishing smacks in dozens.

Alan Goggin, Deputy of the Cinque Port Liberty of Brightlingsea said that he wore the robes and chain of office that his predecessor, John Bateman wore in 1889 when the *Pioneer* was launched for the second time.

Dignitaries arriving in Boy George

He said that one of his duties as Deputy was to collect Ship Tax from vessels using the Port. Having consulted his register he found the *Pioneer* was 115 years in arrears and so the Trust owed the Port the princely sum of one shilling and sevenpence halfpenny! *[Fund raising activities will be put in place immediately. Ed]*

Then, in a simple and moving ceremony the Reverend Richard Salenius, Vicar of All Saints and Saint James, Brightlingsea blessed the ship and anointed her stem with Holy Oil.

Finally with great panache Councillor Jo Ruffel poured a libation of champagne over the *Pioneer*. She said that her Great Grandfather, Joe Ruffel had been her Skipper exactly 100 years ago and she was proud to maintain her family's links with the ship.

The band struck up. Rupert Marks, Trustee, called for *Three Cheers*. The other smacks and barges in the harbour rang their bells and blew their foghorns. And exactly at that moment the *Pioneer* lifted and floated on the tide. She was warped across to the Yacht Club Pontoon and a crowd of well wishers climbed aboard. People had travelled from as far afield as France. Jim Barnard, 91, from Norwich made a keen inspection. He had sailed aboard the Lowestoft Smack *Telesia* in the 1920's. He must be one of the very few people alive who have fished a deep sea smack under sail.

Ashore James Dodds and Janet Harker had mounted an exhibition in the University of Essex Sail Loft. This tells the story of the *Pioneer*. Donations to the Trust and sales of the book, *Pioneer – last of the Skillingers*, at this exhibition and during the journey from Totham totalled £2600 – a wonderful indication of the support for the project.

A reception was held in the Colne Yacht Club. Mac Macgregor opened oysters by the dozen, all donated by a West Mersea Mercant. Brian Kennell, who will Skipper the *Pioneer*, Shaun White and James Green shifted her back onto the Hard.

The Pioneer was home at last.

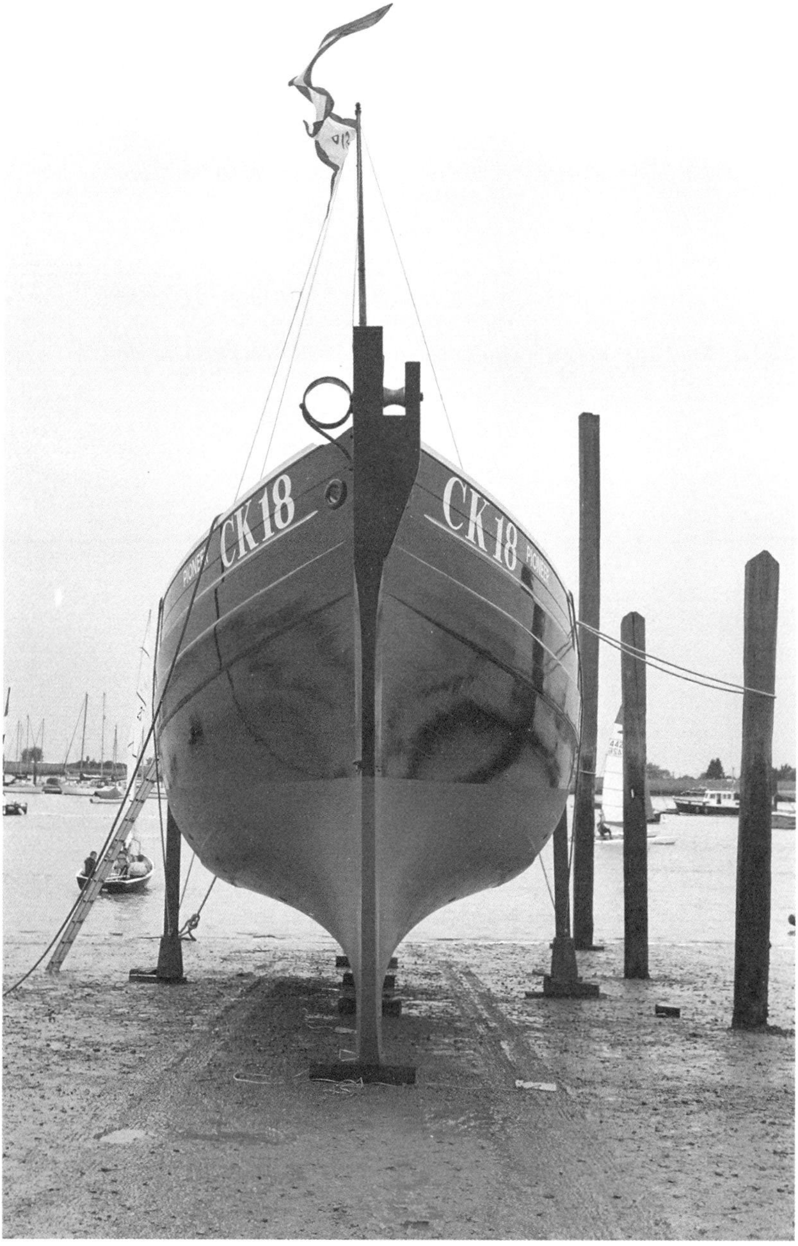

Waiting for the tide

THE BALLAD OF THE PIONEER

by Martin Newell

She was raised from her muddy Mersea grave
In the ebbing days of the century
Stripped of her sails and most of her wales
Long-bereft of her fishing gear
All that remained of *The Pioneer*

And the men who watched this ghost being raised
Thought of the work that the vessel had done
And the work to come . . . the work to come.
There in the bright December sun
The last of her class, was *The Pioneer*

A hundred and thirty years before
Donyland-built, as a fishing smack
She'd joined the elite of the Essex fleet
Bringing the oysters and scallops back
Till abandoned here, *The Pioneer*

Now a fishing smack is a beautiful thing
To those who've an inkling how it's made
And those who'd learn, from stem to stern
The finer points of the shipwright's trade
Might recognise *The Pioneer*

She was built in Eighteen Sixty-Four
Extended later – breadth and length
For deeper seas, which by degrees
Can scupper smacks of smaller strength
And might have sunk *The Pioneer*

But newly-fit with a wet-well now
To keep her oysters fresh in store
She scoured for yields in further fields
Than any she had fished before
Year upon year, *The Pioneer*

And the men and boys who crewed of old
Knew that the shipwright's skill with oak
Was all that they had, if the job went bad
In the murderous folds of the sea-god's cloak
And stared-down fear on *The Pioneer*

From keel and keelson, floors and strakes
Up to the halliards, trees and sails
The parts might bicker and crick and groan
Among themselves in the waves and gales
On a feisty ship like *The Pioneer*

But when the jaws of the starving sea
Were slavering over the decks and mast
They'd pull together, pull together
To cheat the tempest of its repast
One for all on *The Pioneer*

The crew and the ship in the teeth of a storm
Rivalries put away for now
Scarphed together by deadly weather
Port to starboard, stern to prow
All for one on *The Pioneer*

The century turns and turns again
Until one day, on an Essex quay
Absent for years – she reappears
Restored, returned to Brightlingsea
The image of *The Pioneer*

As if the ghosts of all the men
Who'd built and sailed the hardy smack
In every nail, and plank and sail
Had worked as one to bring her back
The Spirit of *The Pioneer*

One curious tale was printed in the Essex County Standard, October 5th 1907:

BRIGHTLINGSEA.
BRIGHTLINGSEA BREEZES.

Last week the dredging ketch *Pioneer* of this place, (master, John Handley), arrived on the oyster grounds in the North Sea. Shortly after the dredging gear had been cast overboard it was found that all her six dredges had been caught fast. The night was dark, but clear, and the weather fine, and the current, owing to the state of the tide, not so strong as normal. While the *Pioneer* was thus held fast by her dredges, another Brightlingsea dredging ketch named *Excellent* (master and owner, T. W. Gunn) saw her plight, and spoke her. Gunn said that as the result of a couple of compass bearings of the French land which he had recently taken, he was of opinion that the *Pioneer's* dredges were caught in the wreck of the *Lady Olive*, a dredging ketch which was run down by a steamer about a year ago, and which belonged to Mr. Joseph Alexander, of Brightlingsea, who is also the owner of the *Pioneer*. Gunn advised the master of the *Pioneer* to hold on until the tide turned, when probably the gear would come clear of the obstruction. This suggestion was acted upon, as the weather held fine and, when the tide had turned, it was found that the *Pioneer's* gear was clear of the wreck below. Strange to relate, when the *Pioneer's* dredges were hove up, they also brought up one of the dredges, with a rope attached, which belonged to the *Lady Olive*. Surely this is one of the most extraordinary occurrences which the secretary of the Smack Owners' Association has had reported to him during his long connection with our deep sea dredging fleet.

✥ **MEMORANDUM.** ✥

FROM

P. T. HARRIS,
YACHT AND BOAT BUILDER,
ROWHEDGE,
✱ ✱ COLCHESTER.

Oct 18 189 7

To *Jos. J. Mather*
Ingringhoe

Dear Joe

The Monara' decks want Caulking I shall be glad if you could come and do them as soon as possible

Yours Truly
Jno. T. Harris
(J King.

SKILLINGING

by James Dodds (great-grandson of W. Pannell)

This excerpt is from the memories of William Pannell (1855-1939). William gave Brightlingsea the Town Hard in 1898, for the benefit of the town and fishermen. He was also part owner of the smacks *Countess* and *Rosa Ann* and owner of the *Water Lily (CK298)*:

"In the autumn of 1881 came news that the Grimsby trawlers were getting oysters in their trawls well down the North Sea off the island of Terskilley. This seemed good to our dredgermen but unfortunately we had very few smacks large enough. Not daunted, our first boat making a trip, I think the *Pride*. Captain Riddett was successful and was at once followed by others notably the little *Dream* and *Emblem* making trips and returning safely. Both these were only just over 20 tons B/M or about 12 tons register, never fit for the job in winter . . . Then came our losses. A terrible time this.

March 1883:	a prolonged gale and there never returned –
	Recruit – Chas. Cann, Master, and five crew
	Conquest – Jos. Barnes, Master, and five crew
	Mascotti – Oscar Salmon, Master, and five crew
12th Dec 1883:	*Pride* – W. Riddett, Master
	Walter & Henry – E Cook, Master
January 1891:	*Glance* – Tom Tillett, Master
	Gemini – John Causton, Master

with all hands (48) and about a dozen hands lost overboard from various smacks over a period of three years."

The reason for lengthening existing smacks to be fit for the skillinging trade is evident from the great loss of life. Larger vessels were needed on these grounds exposed to the full force of westerly gales. A larger vessel can also work more dredges at the same time (up to eight 6ft wide dredges), stay at sea longer, and bring home larger catches. An average catch could yield 50,000 oysters which were kept alive in the flooded compartment called the "wet well", as confirmed in the Brightlingsea Parish Magazine of 1888:

June: "The Skilling season has we fear very near come to an end, at least for our dry bottom boats *(without wells)*. . ."

July: "Always the dullest month in the year as regards our fishery. The largest vessels that have wells are continuing their work at Skilling. Small idle . . ."

In addition, the larger smacks were also being re-rigged from cutters to ketches:

Aug 1886: "Owners are becoming more and more convinced of the superiority of short booms over long ones, both as regards wear and tear and of comfort of the crew, the result being that a large proportion of our fleet are becoming converted into ketches, the last vessel to appear with a short mast on her stern being the *Matchless* CK2"

SMACKS CONVERTED FOR THE SKILLINGING TRADE

LENGTHENED:

Name	Reg no.	Date lengthened	Size stem to sternpost & beam (ft)
Globe	CK73	1836 & 63	33x11 to 45x12
Union	CK33/473	1864	39x12 to 49x14
Antelope		1864	58x14 to 73x17
Palace	CK57	1867	53x14 to 57x16
Pride		1871	50x14 to 52x14
Perfect	CK36	1874	46x12 to 53x13
Countess	CK14	1877	65x15
Gemini	CK119	1880	50x13 to 59x13
Test	CK5	1880	52x13 to 58x14
Glance		1881	52x14 to 59x14
Norman	CK42	Mar 1881	50x13 to 59x14
Pearl	CK113	1882	47x13 to 55x13
Orion		1882	48x13 to 59x14
Vestal	CK4	1885	52x13 to 60x14
Lady Olive	CK95	Aug 1884	51x13 to 61x14
Heiress	CK29	Nov 1885	65x15
Guide	CK3	June 1886	48x13 to 63x16 (71ft overall)
Gipsy Queen	CK20	Sept 1886	69x15
Leader	CK3	1886	48x13 to 63x16
Pioneer	CK18	1889	53x13 to 64x15 (70ft overall)
Express	CK231	1889	42x12 to 48x12
Rosa Ann		1897	40x12 to 49x14

WELLS FITTED:

Name	Reg no.	Date	Size
Lady Olive	CK95	Aug 1884	
Heiress	CK29	Nov 1885	
Countess	CK14	Aug 1886	(costing £400.)
Guide	CK3	June 1886	
Gipsy Queen	CK20	Sept 1886	
Majestic	CK47	Aug 1887	57x15
Excellent	CK30	Aug 1887	63x17
First	CK27	Aug 1887	55x14
Norman	CK42	Aug 1887	
Pioneer	CK18	1889	

RE-RIGGED TO KETCH:

Name	Reg no.	Date	Size
White Rose		1885	
Swift		1885	
Vestal		1885	
Test		Oct 1885	
Matchless		Aug 1886	
Lady Olive		Feb 1886	
Gypsy Queen	CK20	Sept 1886	
Norman	CK42	Mar 1887	
Choice		1888	
Pioneer	CK18	1889	
Majestic	CK47-59	1897	
Christabel	CK66	1897	
Vanduara	CK26	Jan 1897	60x15

The *Excellent* CK30 (launched 1883, see photo p31), *Majestic* CK47 (launched 1883, see photo p33) and *Hilda* CK10 (launched Aug 1886, see photo p16) were some of the few vessels built as a ketches at the Aldous Shipyard in Brightlingsea.

LARGE SMACKS MENTIONED IN BRIGHTLINGSEA PARISH MAGAZINE 1883 - '90S

with details from the Mercantile Navy List 1883 and the 1893 Fishing Register

NAME	TONS	YEAR BUILT	SIZE (ft)	RIG
Pride	23/28	1857 B/sea	50x14 to 52x14	Cutter
Walter & Henry	36	1878 Rye		
White Rose	35	1877 R.Aldous	58x16	Cutter to Ketch
Crusader	50	1868 Grimsby		Dandy
Dauntless	20	1863 E Aldous	49x13	Cutter
Orion	26	1869 E Aldous	48x13 to 59x14	Cutter
Delight	30	1866 Jersey	53x15	Cutter
Two Sisters CK37	27	1863 Jersey	50x15	Cutter
Two Sisters CK65	20	1861 B/sea	50x10	Cutter
Four Brothers	26	1823		
Badger	44	1852 Yarmouth		
Energy	21	1865 B/sea	49x13	Cutter
Kestrel	20	1866 E Aldous	50x13	Cutter
Aid	22	1853 Ipswich		
Miranda	20	1885 R Aldous		Cutter
Moss Rose	27	1885 R Aldous		Yawl
Glance	24/29	1862 E Aldous	52x14 to 59x14	Cutter
Ada	40	1881 Dover		Ketch
Topaz	32	1855 Littlehampton		
Dream	18	1866 E Aldous	48x13	Cutter
Velocity	25	1864 B/sea	55x14	Cutter
Rosa Ann	20-23	1863 J Aldous	40x12 to 49x14	Cutter
Swift		1808 Blackwall		Dandy to Ketch
Emblem	16	1865 B/sea	46x12	Cutter
Spray	22	1843 B/sea		Cutter
Recruit	23	1864 B/sea	51x13	Cutter
Mascotte				Lugger
Conquest	21	1866 B'sea	50x13	Cutter
Matchless CK2	28	1866 Jersey	53x15	Cutter to Ketch
Leader/Guide CK3	24-40	1854 B/sea	48x13 to 63x16	Ketch
Vestal CK4	22/29	1864 R Aldous	52x13 to 60x14	Cutter to Ketch

(Listed below are only some of the large smacks registered to Colchester. The 1893 Fishing Register lists 90 1st class Smacks, all of which could have been employed in deep sea dredging.)

OTHER NOTES	END
Lengthened 1871 Sprang a serous leak on way to Skilling Oct 1883	Missing 1883 Lost Dec 1883
Skilling	Lost Dec 1883
Skilling	To Ramsgate 1885
Stowboating & salvaging	Broken up 1906
Lengthened 1882	Run down Dec 1885
	Lost near Terschelling Feb 1883
Fitted out for Skilling since leaving off stowboating 1886	Lost 1888
Sunk in collision in the Thames 1888	
Skilling Jan 1885	Sold to Norway 1894
From Woodbridge	
Joined Skilling Fleet June 1885	
Stowboating 1885	Run down 1885
Scolloping April 1886	Broken up 1916
Stowboating	
Stowboating	
Stowboating	
Lengthened 1881 E Aldous lost all dredging gear Oct 1883	Lost all hands 1891
Arrived from south coast and fitted out for Skilling Feb 1886	Broken up 1916
After loss of trawl in 1886 goes to join Skilling Fleet	
One of the first Skillingers	Sold to Dover 1892
Scolloping Sept 1886	
(Held by French Customs 1886)	Broken up 1892
Scolloping Sept 1886	
Skilling 1885. Lengthened	Lost Terschelling 1894
One of the first Skillingers	Sold to Iceland 1893
Skilling April 1888	
Master Chas Cann	Lost in north Sea Mar 1883
Master Oscar Salmon	Lost all hands Mar 1883
Master Jos Barnes, Owner J Cross	Lost all hands Mar 1883
Came to B'se 1883. Made a ketch Aug 1886.	Sold to Portsmouth 1900
Lengthened and fitted with a well	
Root & Diaper 1886. 63tons 71ft x 16ft beam	
Made a Ketch 1885. Fitted out for Skilling since 1886	Broken up 1914

NAME	TONS	YEAR BUILT	SIZE (ft)	RIG
Test CK5	21-29	1863 E Aldous 52x13 to 55 x14		Cutter
Hilda CK10	40	1886 R Aldous	58 x16	Ketch
Welcome CK11to470	24	1863 E Aldous	52x14	Cutter
Volunteer CK12	28	1860 E Aldous	54 x10	Cutter
Countess CK14	40	1873 Newhaven	65 x15	Ketch
Pioneer CK18	23-32	1864 E. Donyland		Cutter to Ketch
Gipsy Queen CK20	28-37	1855 Jersey		Cutter to Ketch
Honour CK21	21	1864 B/sea	52x13	Cutter
Vanduara CK26	36	1880 R Aldous	60x15	Cutter to Ketch
First CK27	31	1852 Jersey	55x14	Ketch
Heiress CK29	27-37	1865 Jersey		
Excellent CK30	39	1883 R Aldous	63x17	Ketch
Union CK33 to 473	16-21	1842 B/sea	39x12 to 49x14	Cutter
Norman CK42 to 475	22-29	1873 B/sea	50x13 to 59x14	Cutter
Majestic CK47 to 59	28	1884 R Aldous	57x15	Ketch
Palace CK57	28	1861 E Aldous 53x14 to 57x16		Cutter
Emma CK58	70	1830 Mistley		Dandy to Ketch
Christabel CK66	34	1869 E Aldous	61x15	Cutter to Ketch
Express CK67 to 455	26	1855 B/sea	52x14	Cutter
Billow CK69	21	1864 B/sea	51x13	Cutter
Globe CK73	16-18	1805 Wivenhoe 33x11 to 45x12		Cutter
Ex Care CK95 Lady Olive	24-28	1864 Wenlock 51x13 to 61x14		Cutter to Ketch
Ripple CK99	24	1863 B/sea	54x14	Cutter
Leith CK115	56	1845 Holland. Rebuilt 1869		Dandy
Gemini CK119	26	1866 Wenlock	59x13	Cutter
Viscountess CK129	25			Yawl
Pearl CK133	17-22	1867 B/sea	47x13 to 55x14	Cutter to Yawl
Bee CK194	54	18 - Rye		
Express CK231	13-16	1858 Aldous	42x12 to 48x12	Cutter
Hawthorn CK400	58	1867 Harwich		Cutter to Ketch
Ella CK413	20	1860 B/sea	49x13	Cutter
Fiona CK233		1884 Jersey		Ketch

Lengthened 1880. Stowboating then Skilling March 1886. Broken up1901

Built as a Ketch. First voyage Skilling Aug 5 1886

Scolloping March 1886

Joined fleet 1886 from Harwich

Lengthened by W Puxley 1877 at Rowhedge.

Well put in 1886 at Aldous. Coasting   Sold to Whitstable

Lengthened and well put in 1888/89 Aldous

Made into a ketch 1886 at Aldous

First trip as a well vessel 26 Oct 1886

Scolloping March 1886

Left off stowboating 1886

Made a Ketch 1887. Skilling

Scolloping March 1886   Ran down 1897

Lengthened and well put in 1885 Wivenhoe

Well put in Sept 1887

Lengthened 1864. Scolloping Sept 1886 (Held by French Customs 1886)

Lengthened 1881. Made Ketch March 1886.

Well put in Aldous Aug 1887. Skilling Mar 1886.   Store Hulk 1899

Stowboating then Skilling Mar 1886. Scalloping 1887.

Well put in Aldous Aug 1887   Closed 1884

Lengthened 1867. Joined Skilling fleet July 1885.   Scuttled 1893

Scolloping Mar 1886   1893 Closed. Became CK439

Sold in 1887 for £175.00   Broken up 1904

Coasting Aug 1884, Stowboating then

Skilling March 1886. Coasting 1893-4   Closed 1895. Wrecked 1911

Scolloping March 1886   1895 Closed. Broken up1905

Scolloping March 1886   1898 Closed. Broken up 1898

Lengthened 1836 & 65 Stowboating Oct 1887   Broken up 1902

Lengthened & fitted with well Aldous Aug 1884

Ketch 1886. Stowboating then Skilling Mar 1886.   Run down 1907

Scolloping Sept 1886   7.3.02 changed to CK372

From Grimsby joined dredging fleet 1884.

1st to have steam gear for hauling up dredges   Sept 1890 to Portsmouth

Lengthened 1880. Stowboating

then Skilling March 1886   Lost Jan 1891

First voyage Skilling April 23 1887

Lengthened R Aldous 1882   1897 Closed

Joined fleet April 1889   Sold to Denmark 1904

Lengthened 1889 Scolloping March 1886

Ex Harwich Cod Smack   Lost 1902

Scolloping March 1886   1895 Closed

The last Skilling trip 1931

LIST OF ILLUSTRATIONS

page

2: Blessing the Hard . . . . *(Douglas Went)*

3: Pioneer . . . . *(linocut by James Dodds)*

5: Pioneer at Sea . . . . *(linocut by James Dodds)*

6: Pioneer in transit . . . . *(Den Phillips)*

8: Smack Dock . . . .*(linocut by James Dodds)*

10: Sail Plan . . . . *(David Cannell)*

12: Heiress on Brightlingsea Hard

16: Hilda . . . .*(John Leather)*

19: Scolloping Dredge

20: Vanduara . . . . *(Diana White)*

22: Map showing Brightlingsea and Terschelling

26: Well Plan

28: Peter Harris . . . . *(Nottage Maritime Institute)*

31: Pioneer, Lady Olive & Excellent

33: Majestic at Whitehaven . . . . *(West Mersea Museum)*

34: Essex, Grimsby & Dover smacks at B'sea . . . . *(Colchester Museum)*

36: Colchester Shipping Register . . . . *(P.R.O.)*

39: Pioneer at Brightlingsea, 1900s . . . . *(Shaun White)*

43: Pioneer at West Mersea . . . .*(West Mersea Museum)*

44: Colchester Shipping Register . . . . *(P.R.O.)*

46: Colchester Shipping Register . . . . *(P.R.O.)*

48-9: Thomas Brassey II, Robert Aldous, Erney Beere

49: Joseph Martin Eagle . . . . *(Robert Johnson)*

50: Tom Poole and the Colne River Police . . . . *(Peter Fisher)*

50-1: Victor Mitchell, Joseph Ruffle, William White

52: Mortgage taken out by J.Alexander to buy Pioneer *(Pioneer Sailing Trust)*

55: Pioneer 1998 . . . . *(Brian Kennell)*

57: In the mud . . . . *(Shaun White)*

61: With air bags, Nov 1998 . . . .*(Robert Simper)*

64: Lines Plan . . . . *(David Cannell)*

66: On the lorry, Jan 1999 . . . .*(Den Phillips)*

68: Pioneer's old bones . . . . *(Den Phillips)*

71: Surveying, Mar 1999 . . . .*(Brian Kennell)*

72: Great Totham, Aug 1999 . . . .*(Brian Kennell)*

74: Fitting the new keel . . . . (*Rupert Marks*)
75: Marking out a floor timber . . . . (*Brian Kennell*)
77: Midship futtock frames in position . . . . (*Shaun White*)
78: New and Old . . . .(*Brian Kennell*)
81: "Boil-in-the-bag". . . . . (*Mervyn Maggs*)
82: Midships, showing the well stringers. . . . . (*James Dodds*)
85: Midships, well bulkheads . . . . (*Mervyn Maggs*)
86: New deck . . . . (*James Dodds*)
87: The bow, 2002 . . . . (*Mervyn Maggs*)
    Details of new deck, fitting gammon iron to stem head. . . . .(*James Dodds*)
89: "All Painted up" with original fishing registration no. . . . . (*M Maggs*)
90: Emerging from the shed. . . . . (*Mervyn Maggs*)
91: Waiting for her police escort . . . .(*Charles Harker*)
92: Parked up for a few days in front of Colchester Castle . . . . . (*James Dodds*)
93: Offloading onto Brightlingsea Town Hard . . . .(*Lyn Mathams*)
94: Brian beginning to get a feel for her in the water . . . .(*Mervyn Maggs*)
95: Pioneer in her winter berth. . . . . (*Catherine Dodds*)
95: Shaun and Brian making the main mast . . . . (*James Dodds*)
96: *Pioneer* on the Hard . . . . (*linocut by James Dodds*)
98: Stuck in the field at Scripps Farm. . . . .(*Mervyn Maggs*)
100: Outside Colchester Castle. . . . . (*Mervyn Maggs*)
101: Passing All Saints, Brightlingsea. (*Lyn Mathams*)
102: Alan Goggin, Deputy of the Cinque Port Liberty.
     Mary Falk, Alan Goggin, Janet Russell Mayor of B'sea,
     Councillor Jo Ruffel, Rupert Marks & Charles Harker . . . . .(*Mervyn Maggs*)
     Dignitaries arriving in Boy George. . . . . (*Mervyn Maggs*)
103: Speeches. Councillor Jo Ruffel pouring champagne over
     stem head from one of William Pannell's sailing cups. . . . .(*Mervyn Maggs*)
104: View of the launch from the water. . . . . (*Mervyn Maggs*)
106: Rupert's Three Cheers . . . . (*Mervyn Maggs*)
107: Waiting for the Tide . . . . (*Mervyn Maggs*)
110: *Pioneer, In Frame* . . . . (*linocut by James Dodds*)
111: P Harris Memorandum . . . .(*from the Harris family*)
120: *Pioneer, Deck Beams* . . . . (*linocut by James Dodds*)

Showing the deck beams ready for the decking